PRAISE FOR *ENTREPRENEUR RX*

Over the thirty years of my professional involvement with physicians as executive director of the Arizona Medical Association, I witnessed an evolution in medicine that welcomed physician entrepreneurial opportunities both for direct patient care as well as businesses that benefited from having leadership with physician medical expertise. John Shufeldt is a highly regarded emergency physician who understands great physician leaders are first, great physicians. This book sets forth a working paradigm, based on his experiences and success, designed to encourage physician involvement in entrepreneurial opportunities for the betterment of quality patient care that carries over to a variety of business models. If you are a physician and this is your focus, this book is required reading written by a true expert.

—Chic Older, MHA

Physicians often find the ideas of entrepreneurship and business development daunting and overwhelming as not within their realm of expertise. In doing so, they neglect their intellectual skills and work ethic honed over years of training and clinical practice. Dr. Shufeldt merges his clinical and business acumen with an easily readable style to make this journey accessible to all. While this is his "I wish I had it years ago" book, the reader is the beneficiary of his successes (and failures!). I would encourage any physician interested in undertaking non-clinical endeavors to spend a few hours with Dr. Shufeldt—the time will be well worth the investment.

—Sudhen B. Desai, MD, FSIR (@SBD_IR)

Director, Society of Physician Entrepreneurs

Chief Editor, Interventional Radiology, CSurgeries.com

Scientific Advisory Board, American Society of Pharmacovigilance

ENTREPRENEUR

R_X

JOHN SHUFELDT

MD, JD, MBA, FACEP

ENTREPRENEUR

Rx

THE PHYSICIAN'S GUIDE TO

STARTING A BUSINESS

ForbesBooks

Published by ForbesBooks, Charleston, South Carolina.
Member of Advantage Media Group.

ForbesBooks is a registered trademark, and the ForbesBooks colophon is a trademark of Forbes Media, LLC.

Printed in the United States of America.

10 9 8 7 6 5 4 3 2 1

ISBN: 978-1-950863-24-2
LCCN: 2021903014

Book design by Megan Elger.

This publication is designed to provide accurate and authoritative information in regard to the subject matter covered. It is sold with the understanding that the publisher is not engaged in rendering legal, accounting, or other professional services. If legal advice or other expert assistance is required, the services of a competent professional person should be sought.

Advantage Media Group is proud to be a part of the Tree Neutral® program. Tree Neutral offsets the number of trees consumed in the production and printing of this book by taking proactive steps such as planting trees in direct proportion to the number of trees used to print books. To learn more about Tree Neutral, please visit **www.treeneutral.com**.

Since 1917, the Forbes mission has remained constant. Global Champions of Entrepreneurial Capitalism. ForbesBooks exists to further that aim by bringing the Stories, Passion, and Knowledge of top thought leaders to the forefront. ForbesBooks brings you The Best in Business. To be considered for publication, please visit **www.forbesbooks.com**.

To all the caregivers on the front lines who sacrificed so much and worked so tirelessly during 2020. You are my heroes and I am forever grateful to share this bond with you. Strong work!

Check out johnshufeldtmd.com for more
information on building your business.

CONTENTS

FOREWORD xiii

INTRODUCTION 1

CHAPTER ONE 7
START THE JOURNEY AND NAIL THE RIGHT IDEA

CHAPTER TWO 27
BUY AND STRUCTURE A BUSINESS

CHAPTER THREE 51
START SMART, STAY LEAN

CHAPTER FOUR 63
DEFINE YOUR TARGET AUDIENCE

CHAPTER FIVE 81
CRAFT A ONE-PAGE BUSINESS PLAN

CHAPTER SIX 89
NAME AND BRAND YOUR BUSINESS

CHAPTER SEVEN 103
MONEY MATTERS

CHAPTER EIGHT 125
CULTURE, EMPLOYEE RELATIONS, AND LEADERSHIP

CHAPTER NINE 141
MANAGE METRICS

CHAPTER TEN 155
PROMOTE YOUR BUSINESS

CONCLUSION 167

JOHN'S 21 RULES (AND COUNTING) 175

CURBSIDE CONSULTS 177

ACKNOWLEDGMENTS 187

FOREWORD

P hysician and other healthcare professional entrepreneur-ship is the pursuit of opportunity under VUCA (volatile, uncertain, complex, ambiguous) conditions with the goal of creating biomedical stakeholder defined value through the design, development, deployment, and dissemination of innovation using a viable business model.

The urgency of controlling the COVID epidemic has energized undergraduates, physicians and other healthcare professionals to close the gaps, dysfunctions, and inequities in international health-care systems like few other times in our history. US medical school applications are at an all-time high.

However, providing those interested in physician entrepre-neurial technopreneurship and care delivery with the knowledge, skills, abilities, and competencies (as well as the resources, networks, mentors, peer-to-peer support and non-clinical career guidance) is a challenge if we are to create physician entrepreneurs at scale.

Entrepreneur Rx: The Physician's Guide to Starting a Business is therefore a welcome and timely addition to the growing numbers of volumes on medical entrepreneurship written to educate, inform, entertain, and guide undergraduates, healthcare professional students, and practitioners interested in perfecting the art of healthcare innovation and entrepreneurship.

As a senior practicing emergency medicine physician and serial care delivery entrepreneur, Dr. John Shufeldt skillfully guides readers through the landmines along the biomedical innovation pathways with multiple examples of successes and failures. Like a skilled attending physician at bedside, he directs the reader through the complex process of diagnosing the problems that need to be solved and offers tips on techniques to start, scale, grow, and exit your venture, all with the wisdom and clinical judgment gained from experience.

Clinical entrepreneurship, much like medical practice, is learned after many years working under a master. This book will help you avoid the morbidity and high mortality rates of biomedical ventures at a time when we need that the most.

Arlen Meyers, MD, MBA
Emeritus Professor, University of Colorado School of Medicine and Faculty, School of Business
President and CEO, Society of Physician Entrepreneurs
Denver, CO

INTRODUCTION

You're a physician—likely a very accomplished one. You've probably realized in the last few years that much has changed. You're thinking about starting your own business on the side to protect against, well, a lot of things—burnout, a recession, a pandemic, or an injury or illness that precludes you from practicing medicine. If you are like me, you want to hedge your bets.

The purpose of this book is to make you question that decision. Not to stop you from pursuing it, but to make sure you have all the requisite knowledge to be successful.

Before we get into this, there is one thing you have to truly understand. Start-ups are hard. Do not think this is a walk in the park. It is medical school hard. But like medical school, it is worth the difficulty.

> You're thinking about starting your own business on the side to protect against, well, a lot of things—burnout, a recession, a pandemic, or an injury or illness that precludes you from practicing medicine. If you are like me, you want to hedge your bets.

For a bit of background, I am sixty years old and have been practicing emergency medicine since starting an EM residency when I was twenty-six. For the first fifteen years or so postresidency, I worked eighteen to twenty-six twelve-hour shifts per month, and although likely sleep deprived, I did not burn out.

I have started some fifteen businesses. Three have been very successful (two valued at more than $100 million; one, NextCare, had over one thousand employees when I resigned). I am still involved in three, I've sold four, and the others were mostly failures or collapsed during or soon after the start-up phase.

My goal when I started down the entrepreneurial path was not to get out of medicine. Rather, it was to practice longer. I recognized that to remain in practice, I needed other outlets to avoid burnout. Being an entrepreneur has made me a better physician and person.

To be clear, I am far from an expert on anything. At age eighty-seven Michelangelo wrote "*Ancaro impar*" ("Still I am learning") on a sketch he was working on. I realize that, as of this writing, I have at least twenty-seven more years of knowledge to gain as I continue to evolve.

A lot of physicians have a distorted idea about what business is and what it takes before they actually go into business. They see or read about Bill Gates, Steve Jobs, or Mark Zuckerberg and think, *They didn't even finish college—how hard can it be? Maybe I can do that too. I'm smart, and I went way past college.*

Would-be entrepreneurs love to believe that they too will be an "overnight success." Like Ray Kroc said, "I was an overnight success all right, but thirty years is a long, long night."

I was one of these people—someone who minimized the reality of the challenges of starting your own business. And once I got into it, I repeatedly looked back and said had I'd known this or that, I would have been more prepared.

I wrote this book to give a clear picture of the reality of what starting a business is going to be like and to help you prepare for issues you might not anticipate now. I am also writing for myself, twenty-eight years too late!

There is a lot to contemplate. The first thing is the mental commitment. Starting a business takes a lot of time that you could spend doing other things, such as being with your family, pursuing more education, having more leisure time—things that you enjoy doing. Do you have the capacity, the wherewithal, and desire to have it really impact your personal life, social life, or your downtime?

The second concern is financial. Generally speaking, you have to give up one thing to do another, and what you may be giving up is your ability to make money, at least initially. You have to make the mental leap that what you hope to gain is worth all the sacrifice and the effort; or, would you be better off physically, mentally, and economically picking up another shift in the emergency department or working another day per month in the clinic or at your practice?

The next concern is legal. When you open up a business, you subject yourself to potential legal entanglements. You can get sued, you can go bankrupt, you can lose your home. You can even lose your ability to practice medicine, depending on how bad things get. Even if you're baking cookies at home to sell, the health department can come in and say you don't have a commercial kitchen. And then you get tagged. Thus, even some generally innocuous things can lead you down some difficult legal paths.

But there are also many benefits and rewards. And there's only one way to sum it all up—get ready for the ride of your life!

Looking back, I wouldn't change anything. And I've made every mistake in the world. But I've had the time of my life. You'll have a blast too. One of my favorite quotes is "Life's journey is not to arrive at the grave safely in a well-preserved body, but rather to skid in sideways, totally worn out, shouting, 'Holy shit—what a ride!'" So, just keep turning the pages and hang on!

Taking this leap will change your life. Whether you fail or succeed, it will add value to your life because you will gain insight and knowledge and build up valuable traits like perseverance, humility, creativity, and perspective. You'll learn how to manage people, empower them, and lead them from the front—how to be the person charging the machine gun nest who others will willingly charge alongside. You'll learn about grit, tenacity, and so much more.

The experience of starting a business will make you a better person. It'll make you a better physician. What I've learned is if you're not directing your total focus to medicine, you tend to appreciate medicine a lot more. I've never really felt burned out because I had all these other avenues that kept me feeling alive and valuable. I had a purpose, and it wasn't just medicine. It gives you the opportunity to use medicine and the earnings you derive from medicine to discover your other passions and accomplish other things you really want to do.

> Taking this leap will change your life. Whether you fail or succeed, it will add value to your life because you will gain insight and knowledge and build up valuable traits like perseverance, humility, creativity, and perspective.

If I can do it, you can too. That's why I wrote this book.

I have a lot of experiences and insights to share. I grew up entrepreneurial. I put it on hold until I started an emergency medicine staffing company and an urgent care business a few years after I finished my residency. Since the only business training I had ever received was high school typing—which I basically flunked—I went back to school for an MBA. (Never one to stand pat, I ultimately earned a law degree and Six Sigma Black Belt.)

Over the past thirty years or so, I've picked up a thing or two. Hopefully, by reading this book, you can avoid many of the mistakes I made along the way, including learning what sorts of business ideas are best avoided. Here are just a couple of my less illustrious ventures:

- The all-obituary television channel, also known as Dead TV. I figured if people read the obits in the newspaper, why wouldn't they watch the same thing on television?

- The vibrating tampon. Many women get menstrual cramps in part because of a lack of blood flow to the uterus during menstruation. My thesis was if a tampon vibrated at a low frequency, which a woman could modulate from her pocket with a controller, it would decrease menstrual cramps. Turns out, someone had already filed a patent for the very same idea (obviously, it wasn't all that popular because no one's ever heard of it).

Don't misunderstand. I think of myself first and foremost as a physician. I love practicing medicine. Sadly, not every physician does. A 2019 survey by *Medical Economics* found more than two-thirds of doctors reported that they felt burned out.[1] That's a lot of doctors who may not always be performing at their best—exhibiting a "one more (expletive deleted) patient that I've got to see" attitude.

I don't remember ever being that way with a single patient. Well, maybe one—a skinhead with a swastika tattooed on his penis. I remember saying, "Thank God you are so underendowed, or that would have really hurt!"

---

1 Medical Economics, 2019. "2019 Physician Burnout Survey: Results show growing crisis in medicine." *Medical Economics*, Volume 96, Issue 16.

No excuses—I should not have said that and hope to never stoop that low again. But I believe the reason that I have not succumbed to burnout thus far is that I have an alternate life and income stream. My alternative business interests offered me a hedge against burnout because they allowed me to put my creative energies elsewhere. I practice medicine because I love it but also because it allows me to do something else that I really love—building businesses and changing the world.

Like many people, lots of doctors feel they're stuck. This is what they were trained to do, and it's all they believe they can do.

This book will help shift that attitude. I'll discuss how to develop an entrepreneurial mindset and show you how to spot a great business idea. I'll also cover whether to start or buy an existing business or franchise and how to define your target market, draw up a business plan, make certain you're adequately financed, manage your employees and culture to help your business succeed, and create marketing and public relations strategies.

Look at this as your Business Start-up 101 course—a complete overview of powerful strategies and ideas, as well as all the mistakes I have made.

As an entrepreneur I am always reminded of an experience I had many years ago. I was taking care of a person who, unfortunately, was approaching death. I remember looking at him and noticing the expression on his face. It was clear as day—the "If I had only" look, the obvious regret for everything he had wanted to do but never actually did.

As I looked at that dying patient's face, I immediately thought, *My God, I never want to have that look on my face.*

You don't either. So, let's get started.

CHAPTER ONE

START THE JOURNEY AND NAIL THE RIGHT IDEA

'␣ve been entrepreneurial for as long as I can remember. When I was a kid—maybe six years old—I remember going out to sell tickets for a fundraising raffle (I think the prize was a black-and-white television) for the Boys Club where I boxed. I remember putting my arm under my shirt—so only my hand stuck out of my sleeve—and selling the tickets with my one "good" arm. I never said I only had one arm, but people looked at me and thought, "Oh, this poor little one-armed boxer; I'm going to buy some tickets, even though I don't care about the TV." And I sold more tickets than anybody. Who wouldn't feel bad for a little one-armed boy trying to box? Not my best moment. I grew up making and selling candles, cookies and candies, mowing lawns, shoveling snow, and hawking racing forms and scratch sheets for a horse racing track near my house.

The point is, to begin your journey as an entrepreneur, you have to have an entrepreneurial mindset. Every step along that journey hinges on the ability to notice things that an entrepreneur would pick up on and that others might miss. This involves awareness that there's always the possibility of an idea that might change both you and the world around you.

Feel free to use both arms.

> Every step along that journey hinges on the ability to notice things that an entrepreneur would pick up on and that others might miss. This involves awareness that there's always the possibility of an idea that might change both you and the world around you.

DEVELOPING THE ENTREPRENEURIAL MINDSET

An entrepreneur's mindset isn't all that different from most people's mindsets. It's just a matter of processing what you observe in a different way. I call this putting on a new set of glasses.

I think I've met very few people who do not have what they believe is an idea that will help humanity or themselves. It's a question of taking the next step—seeing a vision or having an idea and saying, "You know, if we could only do it this way, the world would be a better place or it would be easier for people to do certain things."

It's a question of following up, of actually pursuing something that you believe will add value or make things better. Everyone has great ideas—successful entrepreneurs have great execution.

For me, back in 2010 one of those ideas was telehealth. During the course of my career, I came to realize that half of the patients treated in the emergency department or urgent care centers I owned did not need to be examined in person. I thought, *Wouldn't it be great if you could be treated using a secure, HIPAA-compliant video connection and see patients on demand for a fraction of the cost?*

Urgent care was another. As I was working in emergency medicine, it occurred to me that we didn't need to see all these people in emergency departments. We could be treating them in an urgent care setting for literally a third of the cost and a lot more efficiently. (This was in early 1993, and urgent care centers were generally unknown.)

That's how an entrepreneurial mindset works. You observe something and start asking yourself questions as to how a different approach or service might make things better. You have a different perspective.

It's like putting on a new pair of glasses. Invariably, you begin to see things another way. You ask yourself, *How did I not know this before? Now I can see things that are worth trying to change.* To me, that's the entrepreneurial mindset.

It's inside you. You may just have to pivot a bit to help bring it out.

Developing an entrepreneur's mindset also involves leveraging your medical training—good news for physicians who feel their background "traps" them in the profession. For one thing, physicians deal in reality and data. So do entrepreneurs—market research, product development, revenue, and expenses, just to name a few. Physicians can become terrific entrepreneurs because the rules of the game are very similar.

Many physicians are also creative by nature—another part of the entrepreneurial mindset. We look for options. When working with a patient, we're always considering alternatives aimed at the best possible outcome. Many times you're faced with a situation that you have to respond to relatively quickly, sometimes with imperfect information, and only at a moment's notice. You have to be able to think on your feet and come up with creative options—quickly. Medicine certainly trains you to be able to do that, to develop the sort of creativity and decision-making skills that really allow people to be entrepreneurial.

That sort of training highlights another entrepreneurial plus. Anybody who completes undergraduate, then medical school, then residency has to have a good deal of grit. People who aren't determined don't survive the rigors. Although I think medicine's become more humane over the last three decades, you still have to be gritty as hell or you just won't make it through medical school and residency.

That makes for the determination that every entrepreneur needs. As I like to put it, if I have a good idea, it's not going to leave my head until I either kill it or cure it, by which I mean, bring it to life.

Lastly, all physicians have a real sense of compassion and genuinely want to help others. I also think many entrepreneurial endeavors look to benefit mankind. If you look at Elon Musk and Tesla, at the end of the day, he's helping mankind help the earth by decreasing carbon emissions. Doctors and entrepreneurs can see and understand all the ripple effects of what they're doing, how it can transform our human experience.

FAIL FAST, FAIL OFTEN

Failing quickly and failing a lot are experiences most every successful entrepreneur understands. For physicians, that's a different story.

Physicians are the captains of their ships. Like Harry Truman said, the buck stops here. We simply are not trained to fail.

But the one thing that any physician thinking of becoming an entrepreneur is going to have to get his or her head around quickly is the importance of failing and failing fast, because you're going to fail at some point. As you iterate a business plan, there'll be a lot of pivots, a lot of intersections. These are minifailures as you progress along the path of your start-up.

There is also the pivot or persevere intersection—whether it's best to keep going and make small course corrections or to continue on the path and gut it out. And if things tell you it's time to pivot, don't continue to spend time, money, and energy. Fail fast, learn, and pivot.

You'll fail even with ideas that you believed were empirically sound. I know. I just recently shut down a business that had been open for only sixteen months, even though my business thesis still makes a lot of sense.

It was an urgent care business in the Phoenix, Arizona, airport. The airport generally gets one hundred thousand people a day going through it. Needless to say, that's more people than any urgent care facility has access to on a daily basis.

Additionally, people at the airport don't have a lot of time. It makes sense for urgent care to be there. People are often sick before or after they travel. They forget their medications. They have anxiety. They're going to a new place and left their birth control pills or some other medicine. All these things that people do all the time.

It seemed like a no-brainer. We had overhead announcements. We had signs all over the airport. With one hundred thousand people walking nearby every day, all we needed was to get just 1 percent. All the pieces we needed to make it work were there.

It didn't. Apparently, people at the airport are in too much of a hurry to leave the airport or to get on a plane. We calculated that all we needed was twenty-six people per day to break even. The most we ever saw in one day was seventeen.

Eventually, I reached a point where I knew I had to quit throwing good money after bad. The empirical evidence was not there to support continuing. So I pulled the plug.

It was disappointing and surprising, but failure is part of being an entrepreneur. Once you accept that reality, you begin to understand the value of failure. It can teach you a great deal, perhaps even more than your successes. And the faster you fail, the faster you can learn and move on from there.

THE VALUE OF HUMILITY

If you are an entrepreneur, it's essential you have determination and grit. But it's just as important to have humility.

First, it's important to be humble so that you can learn from your failures. If you treat failure as someone else's fault or just a matter of bad luck, you're not going to take anything valuable away from the experience. Humble people are open to learning. If you let your ego get in your way, you will not learn from your mistakes. Even worse, you won't tackle challenging opportunities because of a fear of failure.

It's also good to be humble because you're likely going to experience failure and setbacks in all sorts of ego-crushing ways.

Some time back I had an idea to franchise healthcare. I happened to be in Moscow in 1995 and went to a local McDonald's (a two-story glass building, and everyone there was all dressed up). But what was most important was that the food tasted exactly the same. And I thought, *If they can franchise a way to cook food across the ocean in Moscow, no less, why can't we franchise healthcare?* And so I came back and started to put together an entire franchise plan for the urgent care business I had started two years earlier.

I remember the day the first franchise was due to open. I was driving through Iowa with a friend who, ironically enough, asked me, "Why don't you just stick to being a doctor?" As it turned out, it was a valid question.

We had an 800 number to contact the franchise. To check it, I called. No answer. I tried again. Nothing. Finally, about a half an hour later, some guy answered. I asked him with whom I was speaking. He told me I'd reached the Ford proving ground. I said he was mistaken—wasn't this the NextCare Urgent Care franchise? Nope. Click.

To make a long story short, a secretary had entered the wrong 800 number. We had literally hundreds of high gloss brochures, costing ten dollars apiece, with the wrong number. Finally, after a week, I convinced the proving ground to let us have this ridiculous 800 number.

Ultimately, the idea never really took off. We franchised to medical people, who believed they didn't need to be paying a 6 percent franchise royalty. They could just do this themselves. And so after a few years, we discontinued selling franchises. There were two reasons: I was a terrible franchisor, and I had picked the wrong franchisees.

But I learned from that. I learned about the dangers of being undercapitalized, of working with the wrong franchisees, and of allowing your brand to be altered. I learned that if you want real control, you have to actually own it. So, moving forward, I went out and raised the capital and did it myself.

If you stay humble, you're open to learning from your mistakes. And you will make them, believe me.

REMEMBER: ENJOY THE JOURNEY

This begs the question: When things get difficult, how do you remember to enjoy the experience? How do you maintain a long-term, healthy perspective when times are tough?

I'm probably a stoic by nature. So I always go back to a simple quote—like Tom Hanks said in *A League of Their Own*, "If it was easy, everybody would do it." And so I always make certain to rejoice in the challenges, even though sometimes it's awfully hard. I've always kind of liked the experience of slogging through something. I like the feeling of directing all my effort and the efforts of others to keep pushing that boulder up the hill. I want this to be hard; I want the barrier of entry to be high. It makes your venture more valuable and rewarding when it works out.

If I can do this, I know you can as well. The fun is in the journey, not simply the destination.

NETWORKING AND THE ENTREPRENEURIAL MINDSET

If you want to learn and grow as an entrepreneur, it's valuable to network with other entrepreneurs. Chances are they'll be happy to share what they did right, what they did wrong, as well as other ideas and strategies.

To be honest, networking was always an Achilles heel for me. Part of the reason was I'm not big on asking for help. The other reason was, with the kind of businesses I was trying to build, there simply weren't any relevant authorities yet. We were pretty ahead of the curve starting an urgent care chain in 1993 and tele-health in 2010. Now urgent care centers and virtual healthcare are ubiquitous.

But it still would have been wise to find more entrepreneurs, particularly people who had built healthcare start-ups, and ask more questions. It would have helped me a lot and perhaps helped me steer clear of some of the mistakes that I made.

So, don't overlook all that networking can offer. Check out entrepreneur groups in your area and online. There are also national groups worth investigating, such as Entrepreneurs Organization (https://www.eonetwork.org/) and the Young Entrepreneur Council (https://yec.co/) for entrepreneurs forty and younger.

CREATING TIME TO BE AN ENTREPRENEUR

I like to say that since I pretty much love what I do, I've never really worked a day in my life. Most days I'd work for free, although there are some rare days in the ED when no amount of money would make it worthwhile.

But no matter how you feel at the moment, becoming an entrepreneur while holding down another job, pragmatically speaking, means you have to be a master at time management.

That generally means you're going to have to give something up. Now, if you're somebody who enjoys watching Netflix five hours a week, that's five hours you can devote to being an entrepreneur. But you're probably going to have to make other sacrifices, such as time in the evenings spent with kids and family or cutting back on social engagements. But, remember, you've taken the time to read this book, so don't be discouraged! Time management is often simply just getting better at saying no to things that do not directly add value for you and your family.

But solid time management can take other forms. For instance, when I started my first urgent care business, I would work at that during the day and spend my evenings and weekends in the emergency department. On top of that, I was going to class for my MBA on Fridays and Saturdays. Frankly, save for the years in law school, I've never again been as efficient as I was during that time. Creatively adjusting your work schedule can open up significant blocks of time to spend on your business.

The point is you can always do more than you think you can. I believe that people only hit about 30 to 40 percent of their true potential. I've found over the years that when I think I'm busting my ass and working hard, I realize I am only performing at about 40 percent of my true potential.

Becoming really good at time management is more than just taking advantage of patches of downtime. For me, I've gotten good at finding ways of combining things. For instance, I love to fly, and I love to read. So I listen to audiobooks while I'm flying the plane or helicopter on the way to work. Additionally, I listen to audiobooks while I run in the morning. Generally, I listen to books about or by people I admire so I can learn from their experiences. They become my virtual mentors, but more on that later.

I combine these things so that I can keep doing the things I enjoy without draining time that could go into building a business or, more importantly, time spent with family or friends.

One of the great benefits of being an entrepreneur is that it forces you to become hyperefficient—with time and everything else. It's the ability to finish doing one thing and immediately saying, "OK, now on to this." As is the case for most of us, the busier I am, the better I am. Starting a business venture while working actually improved my output.

This naturally leads to another topic. You're almost certainly going to have to keep working at your current job while you're building a business—even if you can't stand the job you're in. That's a financial reality for most of us.

But there are ways to make the situation better. Approach your current job as a means to an end—in this case, making it possible for you to pursue your entrepreneurial goals. That alone can make your situation feel less like a dead end from which there's no escape. It's helping build a future.

Remember, if you do build a successful business on the side, it helps you appreciate medicine more, as it did for me. There's a greater sense of balance. That can make what often seems an intolerable job situation less burdensome and frustrating. As I've said, I'm a much better doctor because I'm also an entrepreneur.

THE VALUE OF MENTORS

I've had some mentors during my career, but not in the way you might assume.

For one thing, I did not grow up with mentors. My parents seemed to know no one who could play that role for me. So, there was no network of mentors to turn to.

> I'm a much better doctor because I'm also an entrepreneur.

But I came to discover that mentors come in all forms. I found my mentors in books. For instance, I read a book a long time ago by Michael Lewis called *The New New Thing*. All of a sudden, Jim Clark and Marc Andreessen became my mentors. They don't know me from Adam, but they became my teachers, helping me improve and become better at whatever I was doing. When I listen to Steve Jobs's graduation address at Stanford, or David Foster Wallace's commencement address, I'm being mentored by the best. I read or listen to at least one book a week. As a result, I have had some absolutely phenomenal mentors over the years from whom I have learned invaluable lessons and gained rare insight through their lenses.

As a way to pay it forward, I've tried to be a mentor to others for all of my professional life. I think mentors can be very helpful, particularly in helping you remain focused on long-term goals and perspectives. The takeaway is to broaden your scope and ask for help from anyone you believe has something to teach you—which as it turns out is nearly everyone.

In addition to opening the pages of a book, there are all sorts of ways to find a suitable mentor. Other entrepreneurs—particularly ones with more hands-on experience than you have—can serve as great mentors. Ask others who have had a positive relationship with a mentor where they found them, how they approached them to solicit their help, and what they have gotten from the relationship. If you're a recent graduate, consider a professor whom you liked and respected—their jobs implicitly carry an aspect of mentoring to begin with. Look for mentors with real world experience and who are humble enough to share their successes—and failures—with you.

KEEP AN EYE ON YOURSELF

Developing an entrepreneurial mindset means more than just time management, networking with other entrepreneurs, or looking for a great business idea.

It also means looking out for yourself. And by that I mean your physical and emotional well-being.

We in the healthcare field are supposed to be the gold standard when it comes to taking care of ourselves. Some of us are, often through the grace of genetics, quite healthy. But far too many of us are not, often based on the reasoning (a.k.a. excuse) that we simply don't have the time. If you're a physician looking to build a business, exercise is even more crucial as a way to relieve stress, think creatively, and improve your sleep.

Put simply, take the time to care for yourself.

Taking care of yourself is always essential, but it can take on added importance when you're trying to juggle work as a physician with building a business. You'll need the energy and the stamina, not to mention the mental and emotional strength, to perform well on both fronts.

Fortunately time management can offer a solution. In my case, I like to run, bike, lift, stretch, meditate, and sauna in the morning. In that way, exercise doesn't become an afterthought that can be lost later in the day due to a lack of time or other commitments—by working out first thing, it becomes a priority. I'm up by 4:45 a.m. and usually done by 6:30 a.m.—just in time to start the day.

Also, double up. As I mentioned, when I'm working out, I'm also listening to an audiobook—the time management technique I discussed earlier that allows you to kill two birds with one stone. That way your body benefits, as well as your mind. You're going to need both to achieve the goals you've set out for yourself.

Taking care of yourself means getting out of the emergency department (in my case) and using both sides of your brain. It's essential to change your surroundings to remain healthy.

SIDE GIGS AND ESCAPE OPTIONS

For all the businesses I've come up with, I still consider myself a physician first and foremost. I was born to practice medicine. I can't imagine ever retiring.

That perspective has also helped me as an entrepreneur.

Since I look at myself primarily as a physician, it helps keep my activities as an entrepreneur in a healthier mindset. Although the term "side gig" may seem a bit dismissive, that's what you're essentially doing—at least initially.

That's a workable, beneficial balance. As I mentioned earlier, I've found that my work as an entrepreneur has helped make me a better doctor. In that sense, a side gig makes you better at your primary gig—caring for others.

It's also a useful form of self-protection. By approaching building a business as a serious pursuit that comes second to your medical practice, you're not putting your eggs all in one basket. It's an effective way to dip a big toe into the entrepreneurial pool. Should something go south with your business, it won't be as devastating as it might have been.

That benefit also applies to your work as a physician. Until recently I'd always thought medicine was pretty much recession proof (except for certain specialties such as plastic surgery—people aren't getting their noses done during a financial crisis). I never thought that emergency medicine would be affected by anything. But, as I write this, we're in the middle of the COVID-19 pandemic, and volume in the ED where I work is down 60 percent. (Fortunately, in regard to MeMD, the telemedicine business, COVID has dramatically accelerated our growth.)

There's a pragmatic reason for being entrepreneurial as a physician. You need a fallback position because medicine is not recession proof. I learned long ago that to really be secure, I needed multiple streams of income so I did not have to rely just on medicine. Then there is the subjective reason, which will make you an all around better, more complete human being because you'll develop qualities that may not come naturally to you.

Another part of having a fallback position is having an exit plan from the business you're trying to build. You always should start a business with the exit in mind. How am I going to get out of this? Don't assume that this is a forever proposition.

Instead, approach it as though you'll work the business for as long as you can until you can ultimately sell it, then start again. Hopefully, it gets big enough that you won't be able to continue to manage it yourself, so you hire somebody else to do it and then become basically an investor in a business you started. Then your goal is to sell to a larger company that does the same thing, take it public, give it to your kids, or sell to your employees.

Of course, that's if things go well. But never lose sight of the possibility that things may simply not work out. Give some thought to the point in time when you might realize it's time to pull the plug. Consider, too, a financial limit—think about how much money you'll be willing to commit to the business but not a penny more. That way you can avoid simply pouring money into an idea that simply isn't going to take off.

Know, too, that you may go through several false starts—for all sorts of reasons—before you hit on a winning idea. As I mentioned, I started a virtual medicine business called MeMD in 2010—very early in the telemedicine life cycle. It was a slow going, daily fight for the first nine years. Today we have become the hot commodity—telemedicine has evolved from an unknown to a convenience to a must-have.

Then there are seemingly solid ideas that are never bound to work out. When my son was in college, he had two close friends, both from Italy. One was a purse designer. So they started a purse business in college. My son bought the leather in China and sent it to Italy so they could say it was made in Italy. Then it came back to the States. They were beautiful purses. What my son learned is that no one is willing to buy a beautiful purse for $150 without a designer name on it. I still have about three hundred of those damn things in my hangar!

So, there will be missteps. You, like I, will probably have a lot of 3:00 a.m. ceiling fan talks, trying to convince yourself that you're on the right track. Sometimes you may just need to persevere. But other times, it's important to recognize that an idea just isn't right, or isn't right now. It's critical to know when you should cut bait. Fail fast and move on.

FINDING AN IDEA

All those caveats beg the question: With all sorts of ideas failing, just how do you find a business idea that might work?

Start by being observant. Keep your eyes open and don't have a fixed mindset. If you see something, ask yourself how that might work better, be more efficient, or cost less.

A start-up idea is basically your hypothesis about why your company could grow quickly. Think of this as a three-step process. The first consists of the issues and conditions that have contributed to the problem. You want to find an urgent problem that a lot of people share—and is growing. Ideally, pick a problem that is expensive to solve; this way, you can charge more for the solution. Also, do not pick a problem where you can't find anyone to whom it applies.

The second part consists of a solution that, when applied to the problem, allows the solution to scale quickly. Do not pick a solution in search of a problem. In other words, don't think of something cool to invent or code and then go looking for the problem to solve. I've seen people do this with blockchain. They think, *The technology is cool, but how can we apply it?* Start with the problem, and don't try to shoehorn a solution into a make-believe problem.

Finally, why is your solution going to be successful? This is the hard one. Think of it this way—what is the unfair advantage that allows your idea to be the one that grows exponentially? Here are some possible unfair advantages:

- Founder advantage: You know something that no one else knows or you own the patent.

- Growth advantage: You have the solution to a problem that is growing significantly year after year.

- Product advantage: Your solution is at least tenfold better than any competitor.

- Acquisition advantage: Your acquisition path does not cost anything (i.e., it grows by word of mouth).

- Monopoly advantage: As you grow, you get stronger, thereby making it more difficult for any other company to overtake you.

It's natural to share your ideas with your friends—the "what do you think of this idea?" scenario. The problem is that people tend to have friends who are like them. If you like the idea, they may as well. But no one may tell you, "That's the dumbest idea I've ever heard"— which you might need to hear.

It's a better idea to put it out to a variety of people, some of whom are not like you but who are your likely end users. Here's what I did with MeMD. In 2009 a friend called me up and said he was not feeling well. So I told him what I was going to do to help him feel better (called in a script). Then, once that was done, I asked the question "Would you pay forty-nine ninety-five for the treatment you just got?"

From there, I asked myself another question: Who do people call when they don't have a friend who's a doctor? I tried to project myself years into the future by asking what current tectonic shifts I could get ahead of. Mobile phone use was accelerating, bandwidth was improving, and there was a looming physician shortage. I thought, *If this plays out like I think, will it be huge?* The answer was "Absolutely!"

That's the kind of initial thought process you need. Consider the demographics of your end user or your end user in the future.

That also hits on a valuable aspect of finding a great idea—it's often at the intersection of professional interests and passion. For me, my training and experience as a physician are both my profession and my passion. But passion also has a hand in the business ideas I conceive, such as a cost-effective urgent care clinic or a reverse auction for elective surgical procedures. That crossover between profession and passion can lead to some amazing ideas and opportunities.

Frankly, I also like ideas where everyone else thinks it's a bad idea (MeMD was like this). In that case, I convinced myself I knew better.

Conversely, if everyone—friends, colleagues, potential end users—thinks your idea is great, that's just one tiny step toward finding a solid, workable idea. How do you scale it? How do you get it out to the masses?

It comes down to doing extensive market research. Who else has done this? What has their experience been? For example, when I started the urgent care business at the airport, there were probably three or four other airport urgent cares in the country. None of them did well. I dissected why they didn't do well, and I tried to mitigate those issues to make sure my business would be successful.

As it turned out, I had to close the business. But I learned. I found that talking to the potential end user really helps, but what you really need to do is to come up with a minimum viable product—then test it out by finding some early adopters who will be willing to give you feedback. That way, you find out valuable information but don't spend a lot of time, money, or effort on it. You'll also gain a sense of your target audience and their demographics—their interests, their financial situations, and other elements to gauge how receptive they might be to your business idea. (I'll talk about this in greater detail when I discuss the concept of LEAN.)

It can also be helpful to get a sense of the long-term prospects of the industry you're in (the federal Small Business Administration is a great place to start). The issue here is that some business ideas may resist that kind of categorization (just think back to my "Dead TV" idea as one example.) In those instances, feedback from friends, colleagues, and others can prove particularly important. However, remember the caveat—often the best ideas are those that only you understand.

THE "GAP"—MAKING YOUR IDEA A REALITY

So you've got an idea that seems viable. How do you take that idea and move it further into the real world?

The first thing to do is run it by some people who'll force you to think critically about your idea. Number two is putting it down on paper—in Chapter Five I'll walk you through the mechanics of putting together a one-page business plan that will cover many of the issues you'll need to address. This will include the idea, the problem you are trying to solve, competitive analysis, funding, short- and long-term goals, and other practical concerns.

An important part of a business plan is looking at all of the variables of what could possibly go wrong. So instead of putting forth some rosy, unrealistic picture, you think of all the reasons why this is not going to work, all the barriers you're going to have to overcome. And they may come in surprising forms.

Here's one of my previous ideas. A lot of older men take testosterone, but it's often difficult to obtain because you have to make a doctor's appointment, get a script, and fill it. Then it needs to be refilled every few months. The good news is that the vast majority of the men who use it don't abuse it. They give themselves a small dose of IM testosterone every week or topical testosterone daily, following their prescriptions.

I came up with this thesis. Wouldn't it be great if men could go online to get products like testosterone, Viagra, and Cialis? It would be convenient and very cost effective, and they'd receive their medications via overnight delivery.

It would also be illegal, as it turns out. A law called the Ryan Haight Act prohibits people from obtaining controlled substances online. That means physicians cannot prescribe testosterone after a virtual visit. That burned a large hole in my business plan. I realized there was no way of getting around this unless I changed the law, which was not going to happen—at least in the pre-COVID world.

Is finding a great business idea a challenge? Yes, it is. But the good news is, once you find an idea that, after vetting, seems genuinely worth pursuing, the remaining steps will prove a good deal easier. Remember to rejoice in the journey. By pinpointing a great business idea, you've not only identified something of potentially great financial benefit but you may have also learned something about yourself along the way.

As I said earlier, being an entrepreneur can make you a better physician. You've just taken the first steps toward writing a life-changing prescription for your future.

Next up: Should you build or buy a business? And what sort of legal structure makes the most sense?

CHAPTER TWO

BUY AND STRUCTURE A BUSINESS

I love building things. But sometimes the most effective and promising road to success along your entrepreneurial journey is to work on something already up and running.

That question—build or buy—is at the heart of the various ways to start and structure a business most effectively.

In 2012 an urgent care franchise called Doctors Express reached out to me. They had thirty-five or forty centers. They did things a little differently than I had done during my franchise experience. While I franchised to medical providers, they focused on people without a background in healthcare. Even though I thought that was the smarter way to go, about 80 percent of the centers were doing poorly. The franchisees were starting to revolt.

They asked me to come in as a consultant to diagnose and fix the problem. The biggest issues revolved around several incorrect assumptions. The guy who built the original franchise was a wonderful physician whose patients loved him. He partnered with his college roommate, who had a track record of being a very successful franchisor. The original clinic had done well simply because the physician-owner was a great guy. His urgent care was built in an inline location in a small strip mall with poor signage and marginal traffic count.

Based on a sample of one, they encouraged their franchisees to follow the inline strip mall example as a way to lower leasing costs. Unfortunately, as I knew from my previous experience, basing centers in strip mall settings simply doesn't work—there's no real market presence, little visibility, and if there's no large anchor, there's scant walk-by traffic. For confirmation I went around to the different franchisees and interviewed them, and they all said pretty much the same thing—they were not seeing enough patients.

After I got to know some of the franchisees, the franchisors asked me if I might be interested in buying the company. Ultimately, we partnered with a publicly traded long-term care company and followed through on the purchase. We started growing the business in a different way by changing some of the franchise guidelines and developing some of our own centers. It worked out. I exited after twelve months. They went on to sell to American Family Care a couple of years after that.

It was a decidedly interesting switch for me. Having always been a starter, basically an originator, it was a change for me to buy someone else's business.

I tell physicians: if your goal is to tap into a cash flow stream and improve revenue or reduce costs and buy in at or below a market rate multiple of revenue, then buying as opposed to building makes sense. For me, I love building things from scratch, so I tend to default to that. That may not be you. Thus that makes the issue of whether to build or buy one of the first critical choices any entrepreneur has to make.

START FROM SCRATCH OR BUY AN EXISTING COMPANY? AN ANALYSIS

As I said, I like building things. But if I'm going to buy an existing business, I want to be able to think that my participation—the knowledge that came from my experience—will somehow add value. It's important to me to know that my input will be of creative and financial benefit to the end product.

Maybe you're like me. It would be difficult for me to buy a fully baked, up and running, successful business. I would truly doubt how much I could add to that. On top of that, for me, it wouldn't be nearly as much fun.

Conversely, if you're buying something that's failing and believe that you have the tools and time to turn it around, then you might be able to buy at a discounted multiple. Those sorts of businesses have an upside to them in terms of what you might be able to constructively contribute—therefore, it may make sense to invest.

Those are the sorts of questions you need to ask yourself at the outset of your journey as an entrepreneur. If financial success is first and foremost, an existing business may be the best route to take, provided the return on investment (time and money) makes sense. But if your creative contribution in the business is particularly important to you—and, remember, that sort of absorbing involvement can make your life better in all sorts of ways—getting into a business that's already up and running successfully can limit that creative output.

IS FRANCHISING AN OPTION?

That begs the next logical question—what about buying a franchise (not buying the entire company but rather becoming one of many individual owners)?

Many of the same considerations that apply to the build or buy question also hold true here. I think buying a franchise is a good idea for some physicians who may not have the time to develop a business. But you've still got to do your research. For example, if you're interested in buying into a French restaurant franchise, you should go out and research the different French restaurant franchises that are available. You must do market research, even if the franchisor already offers some. You must talk with other franchisees to see what their experience has been with a particular franchisor.

Then it comes down to a simple math equation. You weigh the options—the time it can take for you to build something from scratch or just buy a franchise or business that comes with a time-tested playbook. What's the opportunity cost for starting your own—the time, effort, and resources? On the other hand, what's your expected return on investment (ROI) from buying into a franchise? You're basically investing your time, money, and effort in what you hope will become a cash flow stream.

But, again, there's more to it than simple math. Buying a franchise puts a constraint on your own individual creativity because the playbook is already in place. In so many words, here's the limit of what you can do. For example, Chick-fil-A simply won't let you start serving hot dogs no matter what you say your customers want. Thus it can really inhibit your creativity or ability to pivot.

It reminds me of the movie *The Founder*, which details Ray Kroc's incredible success with McDonald's. This is the way you specifically wrap the burger. Here is the order in which you place items in a bag. This is how you hand the bag over to a customer. For some people, that's fine—"Just tell me what to do and I'll do it, down to the very smallest detail."

But, given their mental makeup, that would drive a lot of entrepreneurs (and me) completely crazy. Even though it may be the best idea in the history of the world, you can't paint the golden arches red. The creative outlet of building a business, of iterating along the way, failing, and persevering, is what I and many other entrepreneurs truly embrace.

If you buy an existing business that is not a franchise, you still have the opportunity to create. You can see something after a couple of months and say, "Well, that's great, but I think there might be a better way to do it." You can make the next creative and innovative step.

When making these sorts of decisions, it's important to ask certain questions, including:

> The creative outlet of building a business, of iterating along the way, failing, and persevering, is what I and many other entrepreneurs truly embrace.

- How much time do you have to put into the business? While buying an existing business or franchise allows you to leverage much of what is already in place, starting from square one is more demanding of your time and effort.

- Just what do you want to get out of the experience? If a quick return on your investment leads your list, an existing or franchise opportunity offers the greatest chance for success. On the other hand, if you want to operate within a cookie-cutter model as little as possible, starting your own business affords much greater opportunity and, for me, more fun.

31

- How important is entrepreneurial freedom to you? If you open a burger joint of your own and discover that two packets of ketchup per customer is just too little, you can toss in as many extra packets as you like. On the other hand, franchises go to great lengths to specify and replicate every aspect of the customer experience—including the number of ketchup packets every customer gets without having to ask for more.

WHAT'S THE SETTING THAT SUITS YOUR VISION?

When thinking about what sort of business could work best for them, many entrepreneurs inevitably end up considering the iconic question: virtual or brick-and-mortar?

For entrepreneurs buying an existing business or franchise, the question is largely moot. If a business already exists in a particular setting, chances are good that's what you have to go with. That's particularly true with franchises—part of their playbook is specifying just where business takes place. They're unlikely to entertain a new-comer's suggestions.

On the other hand, if you're starting a business of your own, you've certainly got more freedom of choice. But the issue shouldn't boil down just to a decision between a physical or virtual presence.

For me, that's not the best question to ask. Instead, consider the specifics of your business idea. What is your idea, and, just as important, where's the best place for it to take hold and grow?

For example, in the early nineties, I had access to ten thousand medical images, including autopsy and histologic pictures. Looking them over, I thought of all the undergrads, medical students, and residents who have to do presentations using images (in the days before PowerPoint). Where were they going to get pictures like this?

So I started a business called SlideSmart. We digitized and collated all the images so users could go online and search by category. Then they could simply download the image or, alternatively, we would send them a thirty-five-millimeter slide of the picture that fit into a carousel projector.

It really was an idea that was ahead of its time, since this was well before the notion of locating these sorts of images via Google. Ultimately, I ended up selling the business and doing fairly well.

The point is that this model would have never fit a brick-and-mortar sort of business. On the other hand, it was a perfect virtual business before virtual businesses were a thing. The model matched the concept.

Conversely, I started a private autopsy business in 1995. We would send forensic pathologists all over the country to perform autopsies, generally in a private mortuary leased for one to two hours. There was no way such a service could be offered online.

Of course, as I write this, we are still in the heart of the COVID-19 pandemic. Just what the aftereffects of the pandemic will be for brick-and-mortar businesses is hard to predict, but it's certain to have a broad impact on almost every business decision, including the question of brick-and-mortar versus virtual. Customer interaction, sanitary procedures, logistics—those and other questions will certainly be examined in a completely different framework.

Even market attitudes have changed completely. A year ago, if you wondered about starting a restaurant, that would have been a perfectly legitimate question. Now, however, you'd be asked about the impact of the pandemic. That sort of significant shift in prevailing mindsets will have real implications for all sorts of business issues, not the least of which is where you see your business occurring and how it will operate.

EVALUATING AN EXISTING BUSINESS

Gauging whether an existing business is a smart purchase involves evaluation of both empirical information and growth and development potential.

Begin by comparing the price with market comparisons. But don't treat that number as a completely independent amount. Look at it vis-a-vis the cash flow stream over time. Taking these together, you can determine whether the overall valuation reflects the asking price. That includes both current value as well as what future value might be after the impact of your involvement.

More specifically, "multiples" can be used to gauge a business's value based on revenue and cash flow. It's a fairly simple formula: multiply a factor such as revenue (useful for e-commerce businesses with a recurring revenue model or EBITDA) by a particular multiple figure—these differ from one industry to another. Information on current multiples by industry is readily available online. One such source is at www.equidam.com/ebitda-multiples-trbc-industries.

From there, consider how the business compares financially with other, similar businesses. As I mentioned, these are known as market "comps" and can be very helpful in determining whether a business's price is in line with market standards. There are any number of resources on the internet that provide this sort of data. A business broker can also be helpful in providing this sort of information. See the next section for more details.

Part of that analysis also takes in what might not be present in the business. Ask yourself if you see opportunities for this business that the current owner missed. Do you see ways to lower expenses that the current owner hasn't noticed? Are there potential markets that have been overlooked? By taking a creative interest in a current business, you can identify what value you may add just by your ideas and participation. This is called accretive value.

Examine as well the circumstances surrounding the sale of the business. For instance, is the current owner getting divorced and needs the funds for legal expenses and other costs? If that's the case, chances are good that you're buying the business at a discount. Even if you do not diverge at all from the current model, the purchase is likely to make sense from a financial standpoint.

Other issues to take into account include:

- Assets. Review a list of everything the business owns, including any equipment and inventory.

- Debts or liabilities. To arrive at a telling figure regarding value, subtract anything the business may owe from the total value of assets. Work with your attorney to decide which is more favorable for you, a stock or asset purchase. There are many considerations that go into this analysis, including tax implications and potential liabilities. I once purchased a group of urgent care centers as a "stock purchase." One week later the business was hit with a large medical malpractice suit from an incident that happened long before we bought. Had it been an asset purchase and had I not specifically included language about not taking on any liability risk from the original owners, we would have been liable for it.

- Location. Is the business located in a setting that may add value? Are other businesses located nearby that may provide a sort of synergy to boost revenue and, as a result, boost value?

This discussion isn't meant to be a definitive guide to assessing the value of any company you're considering buying. Nonetheless, it is valuable to understand the mechanics so you know what to look for.

That said, if you don't have the time or the desire to perform an extensive evaluation—and even if you do—you should consider hiring a professional business appraiser. Appraisers understand market conditions and know the multipliers that are used to value businesses in specific industries. A solid appraiser should also be able to conduct particularly sophisticated valuation methods, such as a discounted cash flow analysis. That's often considered the best and most accurate means of calculating the future value of any business.

I'll talk more about the value of relying on certain professionals later in this chapter. While it's valuable to understand various processes, formulas, and legal requirements, there's really no safe substitution for the knowledge and guidance of an experienced specialist. It also goes without saying that your attorney and accountant need to be on your team as you go through this process.

USE A BUSINESS BROKER?

If you're not familiar with the term, a business broker is a person or company that facilitates the buying and selling of companies. Brokers can assist in determining a fair price, help with various legal and financial requirements, and take other necessary steps leading to a successful transfer of ownership. Some brokers focus on businesses in particular industries or companies within a range of valuations.

In my experience, business brokers generally operate on the side of the seller. Although a broker is technically charged with helping a sale come to a successful conclusion, many of their activities are focused on assisting the seller (e.g., weeding out unqualified or unsuitable buyers).

Thus they have a vested interest in selling you whatever it is they're trying to sell. Like those in other commission-driven professions, they don't get paid if there's no sale. That's why as a buyer I've approached business brokers with a somewhat jaundiced eye. What they're doing is helping best position the business for sale. If they're doing their job, they should help the seller put together a professional, comprehensive presentation for prospective buyers that will allow the seller to obtain the highest price. Although they do add value, they have a focused interest that definitely tilts toward the seller rather than the buyer.

THE NUTS AND BOLTS: BUSINESS STRUCTURE

Selecting the wrong sort of business structure can definitely come back to bite you.

I know all too well. I once made the mistake of turning a business that was originally structured as a limited liability company (LLC) into a C corporation too early. The business was losing money, and after converting it to a C corporation, I could no longer take advantage of the flow through losses that an LLC permitted. That would have lessened my individual personal tax burden by allowing me and the other investors in the business to take our pro rata loss against personal income.

Business entities are creations of, and are governed by, state law. As a result, the challenges faced by owners in one state could differ significantly from those of another. State statutes allow for businesses to be structured through any of the following entities: general partnerships, limited partnerships, corporations (C corporations), limited liability companies (LLCs), and professional organizations such as professional corporations and professional LLCs.

How should you pick the state you file in? If you plan to raise money, filing in Delaware is probably your best choice because it is business friendly and has a long history of settled law.

For the purposes of this book, I'll focus on outlining the structure, advantages, and drawbacks of corporations and LLCs. Approach this as an overview to make you more informed while you work with your accountant and attorney. It's critically important to rely on their judgment and insight rather than just what you can learn on your own.

LLCs are universally considered the more flexible choice. For instance, operating as a C corporation carries a number of requirements and legal obligations—annual meetings, corporate minutes, and maintaining stock books with share certificates, among others. LLCs, on the other hand, generally impose fewer guidelines.

Although the terminology used may vary from state to state, the process for forming a business entity is fairly consistent. States generally require that owners file a single document with the appropriate state filing agent (usually the secretary of state). The document that's typically filed for LLCs is the "Certificate of Formation" or the "Articles of Organization," and for corporations, the "Certificate of Incorporation," the "Charter," or the "Articles of Incorporation." Specific details will vary from one state to another, but all these documents require designating a "registered agent." This is the point person for all official contact.

Regardless of the legal structure, certain agreements are required to govern the relationship between the owners of a business. LLCs address all relevant concepts in a single agreement, which is generally referred to as the operating agreement or LLC agreement. With corporations, the board of directors adopts bylaws. These cover the rights and obligations of the owners, how certain decisions should be made—such as requiring additional capital—and the impact of events such as death or disability of a shareholder.

Tax ramifications are a significant factor in deciding what sort of structure works best. For instance, LLCs have the option to be taxed as a corporation or a partnership. Since C corporations are taxed as corporations, if owners receive a distribution, they're taxed on that as well. That's why you will hear the term "double taxation" when your accountant discusses C corporations with you. On the other hand, LLCs have flow through taxation, meaning that the gains and losses flow through to the owners.

One important point. If you expect you'll need investor funding, your accountant will likely suggest a C corporation. If the company is truly a start-up, initially you're likely not losing a lot of money and the flow through losses won't be enough to matter.

If there is more than one founder, you will each need to sign a stock purchase agreement. Further, you will need to pay for your shares. Since the company is just starting, this amount is minimal. You should also have your stock vested over a number of years, typically four. This is particularly true if you plan to raise money with investors—they want to be confident that you're going to stay in the business, not just up and leave. It also sets a good example when talking to future employees. Since you vested over time, so too will they.

Whatever you do, make sure you include a Section 83(b). An 83(b) allows a taxpayer to "elect" to treat unvested or restricted property as fully vested for tax purposes. This can significantly reduce your tax liability on stock awards.

ACT LIKE A REAL COMPANY

Legal and financial matters are so specific to setting and situation that it's critical to rely on professional guidance. But a few things are an absolute lock—never, ever commingle your personal funds with those of your business, keep meticulous records, set up a corporate bank account, and store legal documents electronically in addition to in paper versions.

It's vital that whatever structure you pick for your business, it is a separate entity. You don't want to give anyone a chance to pierce what's known as the "corporate veil"—personal liability protection against creditors or people who are suing you. A business that's a separate entity keeps your personal assets outside of their bull's eye. However, if you commingle funds—if you create a business checkbook that's also your own personal checkbook—it's pretty easy to pierce your corporate veil. In other words, they can come after you personally. (The other way an opposing attorney can pierce the corporate veil is if the company was set up or organized improperly.)

BUILDING YOUR TEAM (AND RELYING ON THEM)

In many cases, a limited liability company provides the best of both worlds. It affords investors the same legal protections as corporate shareholders while offering the single-level tax advantages of a partnership without the restrictions of corporations. Remember, however, that if you need to raise money, you will likely need to convert to a C corporation or form a C corporation from the start.

That's something of a twenty-thousand-foot view—and with good cause. The reason is, given the nuances and differences surrounding corporate structure from one state to another and accompanying tax ramifications, it's essential to select and work closely with the appropriate professional. By that I mean experienced attorneys and accountants.

However, there is an alternative, at least on the legal front. You can do most of your setup and corporate filings using an application named Clerky or their competitor, Stripe. Both web applications help guide you through entity formation, document creation, and stock issuance. Nowadays, for a start-up, I would save money, time, and hassle and use one of the web applications (and I'm an attorney).

However, if you choose to hire an attorney, make sure they understand corporate law. Moreover, make sure you stay involved in the process.

If you hire a corporate attorney, they will know all the specifics and nuances of the particular state, county, city, or other entity in which your company may do business. The differences from one location to another can be staggering, so it's critical to partner with pros whose practice is specific to your location and, even better, the sort of business you want to build.

Here are just a few of the issues your legal and financial teammates can address:

- What should be handled first in forming your business? Do legal or financial matters take priority?

- What type of legal structure will you pick (LLC or C corporation)?

- Formation documents. What's most important to address immediately?

  □ Articles of Incorporation

  □ Bylaws

  □ Stock purchase agreements and vesting schedule

- What sorts of licenses are required?

- What contracts do you need? Contracts protect your business by describing the rights and responsibilities of parties to the agreement. A well-written contract can reduce the number of disputes that arise, ensure that you get paid for the work you do, and provide a clear remedy if one party doesn't hold up its end of the deal. Your business might need contracts for routine transactions to protect confidential information (Confidential Information Assignment Agreement), to describe employment relationships (generally, you should not have employment agreements—at least at the start), or for leases and other major transactions.

- How do you minimize risk? A variety of federal and state employment laws may apply to your business, and you risk fines, penalties, and/or employment-related litigation if you don't know the laws and stay in compliance. Federal laws range from antidiscrimination laws to health and safety regulations to wage and hour laws. You may need policies and procedures, handbooks, and training to ensure that you don't inadvertently violate them. You must also comply with laws relating to such issues as the minimum wage. And if you employ people who are not US citizens, you may face immigration-related problems.

- What particular or even unusual laws apply to your business? Do certain ones apply just in the formative stage of the business?

Those and other matters like them carry significant ramifications—consequences that make choosing a suitable attorney or tax pro a critical step in your entrepreneurial journey. To help you with that important task, here are lists of issues to consider, as well as suggested questions that you should definitely ask any attorney or tax specialist you're considering:

ATTORNEYS

1. Should I hire an attorney or use Clerky or Stripe?

When I start my next venture, I will use one of these two web applications. I will also use Carta for keeping track of the cap table (who owns what amount of stock). If you're not comfortable with technology, by all means hire an attorney.

2. Where can I find a business attorney?

Start by asking other business owners and any close advisors with whom you already work. An attorney who has the money to land a high ranking in a Google search may be completely ill suited to help your business.

3. How do I research their qualifications?

An attorney fresh out of law school may be inexpensive, but a seasoned attorney who may be more expensive likely has experience with your industry or navigating the nuances of your city and state. That's worth the extra money. A family law attorney can handle a child custody dispute but may not be particularly skilled at setting up a new business entity. As an example, I have been licensed to practice law for fourteen years, and I don't do my own corporate or regulatory work. That is how nuanced and important it is.

Your first step is to review the attorney's biography. If they seem like a possible fit, interview them for the position. Questions you may want to ask include:

- How long have you been practicing law?

- Have you had any ethics complaints filed against you?

- Have you done this specific type of work before? How many times?

- Do you have specific experience in my industry? Issues such as intellectual property, franchise agreements, and service contracts require special knowledge and skill.

- Do you have experience in structuring a business? For example, ask the attorney to describe the difference between an S corporation and an LLC or how much the annual franchise tax is for a corporation in whatever states you may be doing business.

- Who's going to be doing the actual work? Most lawyers assign work to paralegals, but overdelegating can be confusing and ultimately cost you more money. Conversely, you do not want to pay attorneys to perform rudimentary work.

- What's your approach to conflict resolution? Find out how much of an attorney's time is spent in court and how much is devoted to mediating disputes. If they go to trial, will you have to hire a trial attorney?

- Do you work with any competitors?

- How quickly do you get back to clients—and how?

- Can you offer examples of work similar to what I will require?

- Can you put me in contact with a few clients with whom you have done similar work?

- Are you amenable to negotiating your fee? Most will be open to that request.

4. Are their rates reasonable?

"Reasonable" is a mercurial term, to say the least. Partners in large law firms can charge as much as $1,200 per hour. This can lead to large, unexpected legal bills. What may seem like a simple legal question can result in your receiving a ten-page memo and a $4,000 invoice.

Ask about alternate compensation arrangements. Some attorneys are willing to offer flat project rates. Some attorneys may also be willing to cap the amount they charge for a project.

5. How will they prioritize my needs?

Some attorneys may be tempted to sell you additional legal services that you may not need right away. Ask the attorney how they would prioritize the timing of any steps they recommend. For example, can you set up your company now but wait to file for a trademark until you're confident the business is actually viable?

6. Will you get along?

Personal chemistry is extremely important. You're going to be spending a good amount of time with this person. Will you look forward to meetings or dread them as you would a colonoscopy? Is the attorney someone you'd want to develop an ongoing relationship with as your business grows?

7. Meet with several business attorneys.

Talk with several candidates. Most business attorneys provide free initial consultations. That way, you get a sense of different types of services as well as personality types.

Be picky. Remember that attorneys are business owners as well and some are reluctant to turn away new business—even if they are not particularly well qualified. Trust your instincts. Finding a solid fit early on can help you avoid untold frustration and expense down the line.

TAX PROFESSIONALS

1. What services do you provide?

Most CPAs and accounting firms provide a range of services, from assisting with monthly bookkeeping to payroll processing/payroll taxes to audit representation. For the most services under one roof, a CPA is better than an accountant because CPAs can do more.

2. Do you have experience with my kind of business?

Not all types of businesses are handled the same way from an accounting and tax standpoint. Having a firm that understands your field is critical. Make sure your accountant has experience with your type of business, particularly if it's healthcare. Most start-ups use cash as opposed to accrual-based accounting. Cash-based accounting is also used to calculate income tax.

3. Can you represent me everywhere I do business?

Ask if the firm is able to practice in all states where you have a business. Many states have reciprocal agreements, but it doesn't hurt to ask.

4. What are your philosophy and tax planning priorities?

Is this person cautious, assertive, or aggressive about deductions? Your CPA's style and philosophy should match yours. If you're not comfortable, keep interviewing. You need an accountant that plans with you and anticipates your estimated tax liability.

5. What are your fees?

Ask how the firm bills clients and billing options. Most firms bill on an hourly basis, but some firms offer a monthly rate. Ask what's included in a monthly arrangement.

6. How often do you recommend we meet to discuss my taxes?

One primary purpose of having a CPA is tax consultation. Ask how often this person recommends meeting to discuss taxes. You should meet at least annually after financial statements are prepared, and some firms recommend meeting even more frequently.

7. Are you available year-round?

Some accounting firms shut their doors for a month after April 15. You need someone all year long.

8. Who will be doing the work?

Accountants often outsource work. That's not necessarily a problem, but make sure they are forthright about who is doing the work.

9. How do you handle working with multiple entities?

If you have more than one entity under your name, be sure the person can manage them simultaneously—a skill not all accountants possess.

TO PARTNER OR GO IT SOLO?

We've all been there. We know someone who's a good friend with solid character and who shares your entrepreneurial spirit. Should you partner with them in your business?

I've worked with many types of partners. I've had really good partners and some really challenging partners where we've ultimately had to part ways. The problem is that we all tend to want to find partners who are like us. While that sounds like a good idea, I am reminded of the old Henry Ford adage—if two people feel and think the same way about everything, one is unnecessary.

Even though we tend to pick people who mirror us, that's not who you want. You want people who can respectfully disagree with you. You want people with whom you can respectfully fight it out. You want people who will push you in a collaborative way and who have different skill sets than you. Marc Andreessen and Ben Horowitz of the venture capital firm Andreessen Horowitz battle it out over investments. Although they are close friends, they often look at businesses with an entirely different perspective. If you track the businesses they invest in, it's clearly working.

Don't ever downplay integrity and values. Find somebody whose integrity is evident. Even if you know them, do some legwork. Look at their past behavior. Look at the people with whom they associate. Do their words match their values and actions?

Remember, you may be in a ten-year relationship with your cofounder, so getting it right is important. You will have disagreements, so making sure that you can both follow a few rules is key to keep things focused:

- If you have an issue, stick to just that one. Don't bring up past problems. Don't speak with contempt to your partner: "That's the dumbest thing I've ever heard!"

- Don't be defensive. If you disagree, listen to your partner and respond. Take ownership. Talk it out.

- Lastly, no stonewalling. Don't just walk away from problems or difficult discussions.

I've made my share of mistakes picking partners. I once partnered with a doctor who I thought had integrity. Not true. I didn't know about his malfeasance until a patient called me. She was upset about her outcome and a $7,000 bill. As she explained her situation, she happened to mention that she had just made out a personal $7,000 check to my partner—not the business. When I confronted him on it, he swore up and down that he was going to pay the business back. That was my cue.

He subsequently lost his license to practice medicine for an entirely different reason, also having to do with his lack of character. He's never practiced medicine again.

That's an extreme example, but it's essential to take the time to find the right sort of partner. Partnering with someone who's honest and acts with integrity is a given, but a more common mistake is an issue I've raised before—partnering with someone who's too much like you.

I talked about this problem when discussing a new business idea. The same holds true for a business partner. For one thing, like an early-stage business idea, a developing business needs discussion, disagreement, and frank dissent. Great businesses are built not only by partners who support one another but also by those who examine details carefully and aren't hesitant to voice concerns and criticisms.

Building a successful business also mandates people with complementary skills and abilities. If you're great at working with numbers and financial analysis, it can be needlessly redundant to have a partner with precisely the same expertise. Far better to partner with someone who knows his or her way around marketing, social media, or some other component of the business. I am much better at vision, strategy, raising money,

> Great businesses are built not only by partners who support one another but also by those who examine details carefully and aren't hesitant to voice concerns and criticisms.

and building teams, so I always look for partners whose strengths are in operations, HR, marketing, or finance.

Approach your business partner as you would anyone else you recruit for your team. Take all the time you need to find the best choices possible and from there have the courage not only to work with them closely but also to rely on their judgment and perspective.

The right business partner can also trim the risks associated with a new business. That's the focus of Chapter Three.

START SMART, STAY LEAN

Talking about going into business is one thing. Putting that goal down on paper boosts it to a completely different level.

Sales expert Tom Hopkins expresses it very well: "An unwritten want is a wish, a dream, a never-happen. The day you put your goal in writing is the day it becomes a commitment that will change your life."[2]

Writing down your business goals is very smart. But "smart" is not just a description of intelligence. In the context of this discussion, it's also an acronym that can help guide you in crafting and executing a powerful and achievable strategy.

Part of being smart involves pursuing your business goals with the least amount of risk. Of course, there's always a degree of uncertainty to any new business, but the more you're focused on a strategy that's cost efficient and substantial enough to gauge the market's reaction, the more quickly you can be on your way to a business that grows and evolves.

That's the lean part of the discussion. You want to start your

---

2   "What is a Goal?" *Tom Hopkins International.* http://www.tomhopkins.com.

business smart and stay lean as you gain a toehold with your target audience. Applying those principles that I'll discuss in detail in this chapter will help make any major steps in building your business that much more attainable. It's a powerful, encompassing framework that's effective in many situations.

FIRST, START WITH SMART

I've written down my goals for years, using a system that incorporates both short- and long-term goals. The synergy is perfect—as I complete smaller steps that comprise yearly goals, I also build toward longer goals, such as five-year or longer-term benchmarks.

They're personal as well as professional goals. Personal may be practicing mindfulness, meditating daily, reading one book a week, or running at least twenty-five miles per week.

Professional goals include selling a business, starting a new business, or recruiting five new board-certified physicians to staff a new emergency department.

To be honest, I was intimidated when I started writing down goals. Once they were on paper, though, I could no longer make excuses or forget about them.

That's a point I can't stress enough. If you have business goals, write them down. They implicitly become more "real." You gain a sense of obligation to them. They hold you accountable. As you work toward achieving them, you're reminded that the reward will inevitably outweigh the effort involved. You pay attention to your efficiency and strategies to make the most of your time.

In effect, you're setting goals instead of setting wishes.

MAKE THEM SMART GOALS

When it comes to setting goals, you don't want to be merely smart. You want to be SMART.

Consultant George T. Doran coined the SMART acronym in 1981, forever changing the way people establish and accomplish goals. The SMART system clarifies your ideas, focuses your efforts, and uses your time productively to increase your chances of accomplishing everything you set out to achieve.

SMART stands for specific, measurable, attainable, realistic, and timed.

- **S—Specific:** SMART goals must be specific enough so that you'll have a greater chance of achieving your goal. The more on point you are, the better. By "specific" I mean you should know details regarding what, where, when, and why. When starting a business, you should know in detail what the business is (franchise or start-up), where it will be located, when it will open (or, if already open, hours of operation), and why. The last consideration—why—is particularly critical. Why are you doing what you're doing? What's your motivation? Whom do you wish to serve? More about this in Chapter Six.

- **M—Measurable:** It's critical that you monitor your progress toward your goal as comprehensively as possible. That can be as simple as delineating time markers to reach certain benchmarks—if you wish to lease space for your business within five months or raise a certain amount of money by a particular date.

- **A—Attainable:** Even the most desirable goal is of little value if it's clearly beyond your reach. While a SMART goal should stretch your capabilities, make certain to establish goals that are both challenging and reasonable. That can mean a certain amount of revenue by the time you finish your second year of business instead of expecting it immediately out of the gate.

- **R—Realistic:** This is closely related to attainable. You want realistic goals. Pursuing unrealistic outcomes will discourage you. For instance, building a franchise of ten locations within five years is realistic—doing the same within six months is a mere pipe dream.

- **T—Timed:** Time frame builds a sense of urgency—an obligation to stay on task until a goal is reached. Once again, balance challenging goals with a reasonable amount of time in which to complete them. Timelines keep you focused and motivated.

When mapping out plans for your business, it's helpful to consider any decision within the framework of the five SMART components. Not only can they keep you focused, but they can also help you avoid missteps that don't align with the five parameters.

COMPLEX SMART GOALS

Not every SMART goal has a straight, linear path. In fact, many are quite complex, with a number of moving parts. This means the process of achieving your SMART goal can prove more complicated than simply moving from point A to B.

Still, on occasion, it's hard not to become a bit overwhelmed trying to reach a complex goal. To overcome this, I break down every piece of the goal into manageable bites. That lets you experience success in small increments and strengthens your resolve.

A series of smaller steps also affords the possibility of experiencing unintended positive outcomes. For instance, if your complex SMART goal is to incorporate a sophisticated billing system business, one unintended benefit is learning new technology.

Here's a breakdown of steps when approaching complex SMART goals:

- Start with an objective—opening a successful business, for instance. This will be the heart of your complex SMART goal.

- Brainstorm different variables you'll need. Ask others for help with ideas.

- Think through all obstacles you need to overcome.

- Organize variables into groups and identify a theme. Each theme will contribute to your larger complex SMART goal. This also allows you to then create smaller SMART goals. For example, if your SMART goal is opening an urgent care facility, the themes may be:

  - Incorporation

  - Site selection

  - Design

  - Contractor

  - Build-out

  - Health plan contracting

  - Staffing

  - Preopening

  - Electronic health record selection and installation

    □ Revenue cycle management

- Next, identify variables within each theme. For example, electronic health records would include affordability, required training, and access to system updates, among other elements.

- Break down your overall complex SMART goal by writing a SMART goal for each theme. For example, "I want to have an electronic health record selected by a specific date that meets the following criteria."

- Create actionable steps for the smaller SMART goals. Selecting an electronic health record requires multiple product demos, reviews, pricing discussions, and interviews with current clients.

- Map out a plan. Each of the actionable steps to accomplish the smaller SMART goal should align with reasonable dates. This is essential to stay on task.

- Track each actionable step to make sure you're on target to reach your goal.

- Adjust times and actionable steps as you evaluate your progress. Although adjustments can make sense, commit to staying on task and on time.

- Modify your SMART goals when you fall off schedule. Don't be afraid to add more steps to ensure you will reach your goal.

The following diagram offers a visual summary of a complex SMART goal with three themes.

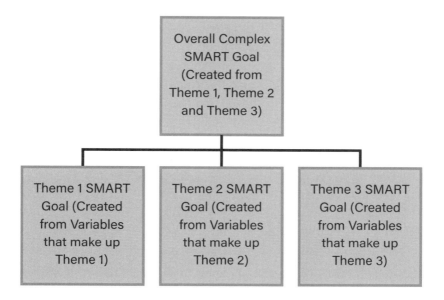

Try to be reasonably flexible when mapping out steps toward SMART goals. Course corrections—the "build the wings as you're flying" mindset—doesn't mean you're abandoning your commitment. Rather, it represents necessary changes to maintain that commitment. You're simply using what you have learned.

KEEP IT LEAN

SMART goals are somewhat abstract. They're undeniably powerful parameters, but they are primarily planning focused. It's execution of that thinking that leads to success.

Many entrepreneurs encounter serious challenges here. Not only do they fail to think things through, but they also don't do sufficient research into whether anyone will be interested in their product or service, whether that market is substantial enough, and answers to other critical questions. Just as devastatingly, they dive into the business far too deeply from the outset. They overcommit before they have credible information and guidance.

That's why a lean approach to the initial steps in your business is an important component of the overall SMART system. If you pursue a lean methodology, you're less likely to fail. Moreover, if things don't work out, you will likely spend less money with less heartache.

Lean doesn't mean cheap. In fact, you may spend more in the early phase to test your hypothesis. Lean prevents you from building something no one wants. Lean prevents you from making serious, costly mistakes. Lean means being efficient. It means a fast feedback loop that allows you to try, fail, learn, and try again—quickly.

Believe me, I went against this approach in my earlier years as an entrepreneur. For instance, with regard to the opening of MeMD—a virtual care company—I made two central assumptions:

One was that urgent care centers would want to expand patient load by seeing patients virtually throughout Arizona, reducing provider downtime, and generating additional revenue. Urgent care centers in the state suffered times where patient flow dropped, particularly in the summer.

Additionally, that patients with minor complaints would jump at the chance to be treated virtually. Who wouldn't want to be seen almost immediately from their own home when they felt sick—and for a very low cost?

No-brainers, right?

Both of these assumptions were wrong. Concerned about decreased revenue, urgent cares were worried that patients would automatically choose the less expensive virtual option. The common response I heard from owners was that they would be cannibalizing their own business.

Secondly, I was wrong about the appeal of virtual visits. In 2010 the thought of seeing a physician virtually was beyond the imagination of most patients. By the time I realized this, I had a fully functioning platform with a large, generally unused provider network and a team of about ten people.

THE SOLUTION: VALUE PROPOSITION AND MINIMUM VIABLE PRODUCT

Mistaken assumptions have put many business ideas into premature coffins—assumptions that ran counter to the lean principles that there's a market for your services.

To have a clear picture of your value proposition, test the appeal of that value with a minimum viable product (MVP).

A value proposition tells prospects why they should do business with you rather than your competitors. It also imparts a clear picture of the benefits of your products or services.

Value proposition focuses on one essential question: What problem does your business solve?

When I started MeMD, our target problems were:

- No one wants to wait for an appointment when they feel sick.

- People would rather be seen in their home versus traveling to a doctor's office.

- Patients want to know the cost up front.

Hence, the MeMD value proposition: A provider would see you virtually within twelve minutes for a flat rate of forty-nine-ninety-five, with scripts being electronically sent directly to the pharmacy. It would be cost effective, fast, and convenient.

Of course, even the most seemingly rock-solid value proposition needs to be vetted in the most cost- and time-efficient manner possible.

Enter MVP.

An MVP is a product or service with sufficient function and features that can be offered to customers. On the one hand, an MVP that's usable enough lets you observe customers' actual behavior with the product or service. That takes your audience research a step beyond mere opinions. Since these are the early adopters, they'll provide ongoing feedback as you iterate through the design phase.

For urgent care centers, one example of an MVP would be leasing a clinic or several examination rooms for a short period of time. From there, have customers use the service and offer their feedback on various elements—quality of care, speed, efficiency, customer service quality, and other aspects.

The idea is to offer users a firsthand level of experience with what you hope to sell them on a larger scale later on. In effect, you're testing a hypothesis. Interact with your users, see how they are using it, and iterate.

Your initial product may suck. A famous mantra is that if you are not embarrassed by your MVP, you started too late. For instance, the founders of Airbnb used their own apartment to test out the idea of peer-to-peer rentals. The first Airbnb did not even have a map feature or payment options. Foursquare's MVP initially involved users by having them check in at multiple locations to earn badges. Foursquare's evolution into a comprehensive city guide only occurred after the initial stripped-down version proved popular. (Of course, there are some industries where an MVP won't work, like biotech, banking, insurance, or any heavily regulated industry.)

Some of the valuable pieces of information and insight an MVP can offer include:

- Are the people receptive to your idea early adopters, or does your idea appeal to a broader audience? Popularity limited to early adopters can be encouraging but also misleading about long-term appeal.

- How educated is your audience? Do they understand and appreciate your product or service, or do they need to be better informed? This can not only suggest how viable your idea is overall but also how soon it's prudent to offer a more completely developed product. Don't try to address all needs on the first iteration. If extensive education is necessary, a quick rollout may prove a disaster. Selling something that has potential but little precedent always takes more time and money than you think it's going to—as opposed to just starting, say, an ice cream shop.

- Are any of your assumptions reflected in customers' experiences? For instance, did you expect price to be the major appeal of an urgent care clinic when, in fact, your audience values convenience more?

- Does your target audience want something more or different from your idea? Is there room for their desired evolution in your current product or service? Are you establishing relationships with a target audience that will last?

A solid MVP allows you to test the hypothesis behind your business before committing significant time and resources. Interviews, surveys, and website analytics are several common ways to gather this critical feedback.

Consider the metrics you'll use to determine whether an MVP is worth pursuing or abandoning. For instance, with an urgent care center, it could be something as simple as patient volume, percentage of return visits, and door-to-door time.

Don't fall in love with your MVP. The goal is to get something out quickly with enough functionality to attract enough users so you can learn from them. Remember, you should be embarrassed.

It's also important to apply one aspect of SMART to your MVP experiment—establishing a date by which you decide whether to continue with the product as it is, tweak it, or cut bait. Do you persevere if your hypothesis is somewhat correct? Or do you have to pivot or iterate in some manner? Know that as you gather end user information, you will have to continue to iterate and pivot accordingly.

A lean approach can also make pivots, particularly significant ones, more viable. For example, when we built the airport urgent care center, we fashioned it in such a way that someone else could easily go in and tear down a few walls and use it for something else.

Employing both the SMART and lean strategies lets you accomplish a number of significant goals in your business's early stages. You can determine whether your business hypothesis is, in fact, a workable idea with potential. Moreover, you can do so quickly and cost effectively.

> A lean approach can also make pivots, particularly significant ones, more viable.

In particular, the SMART methodology is a strategy that can be employed throughout the lifespan of your business. You'll likely find there are few tools that are as applicable and effective, no matter what sort of business you're in.

And, no matter the sort of business you have in mind, you need to identify your target audience—those people at the core of your market. That's the crux of Chapter Four.

DEFINE YOUR TARGET AUDIENCE

I dentifying and reaching your target audience are absolutely critical steps—as important as most anything in the early stages of your entrepreneurial adventure. That said, the bottom line is, if you have really found *the* solution to a problem that's accelerating, you should not have a problem finding your audience.

That's inevitably true, even amid something as widespread and impactful as the COVID-19 pandemic.

I've known a particular intensive care doctor for many years. He's a brilliant guy, very funny, but also a great source of business ideas. Here's one we considered during the late summer of 2020—when businesses, schools, and other entities were beginning to take the initial steps toward resuming some semblance of normal life.

My friend mentioned the importance of a system or protocol with which businesses could reopen safely. His idea involved examining a number of factors—consumer-based demographics, store density, number of employees that could operate the business safely, air quality, prevalence of the virus in the surrounding community, and other issues. Ultimately, the idea was to offer a service to businesses that quantified their overall level of risk.

At first, the idea seemed spot on—we even went so far as to consult with an epidemiologist about any necessary mathematical analyses.

But there was one unresolved question: Would anyone actually want to buy it? What was the target audience, how large might it be, and would it be substantial enough to make the concept attractive in the real world?

As I write this, we still haven't made up our minds, but one issue stands out—would a risk assessment designed to be as realistic as possible actually attract more people to the businesses that purchased it? And if it did lure more customers, wouldn't that inherently change the risk level since more people would be inside a particular location?

That highlights the importance of identifying your business's target audience. Do you have a great idea that no one will actually buy? Moreover, is your idea great but before its time? Do you have a great solution that lacks an actual problem?

I've dealt with this repeatedly with regard to urgent care clinics. It always made complete sense. Who wants to go to the emergency room when you can pay a quarter as much for the same treatment at an urgent care facility? Not very long ago, that was also true for telemedicine—a terrific concept, but of little appeal only a few years ago. Now, thanks in part to COVID, it is accelerating rapidly.

Those and other issues make identifying your target market or audience particularly challenging but no less essential.

A CORE CHALLENGE: EDUCATING THE MASSES

Why certain business ideas explode into success while others wither and disappear can be traced to many issues. Again, timing is one. A business that initially flops can become wildly successful in a different time and circumstance.

Pricing is another issue. What consumers are willing to pay at a certain price point can be utterly rejected at another price level. There's a reason why a certain service costs $99.95 instead of $100. Perception is everything.

These sorts of challenges can be distilled down into one central component—the importance of educating the people who might be interested in buying your product or service. They have to understand it to find it attractive, and that education costs money.

That can be a significant issue to overcome. First, some ideas just seem too foreign to many consumers. That was the case with telemedicine. Many would-be users simply couldn't process the concept of being treated by a doctor without any sort of physical contact.

That ties in with timing. Often, getting people to understand what your product or service is about can be impacted by surrounding events. Although the pandemic certainly was a catalyst for the growth of telemedicine, it's safe to say that the idea was trending toward greater acceptance prior to that. Cocooning, remote work, and other trends made telemedicine less of an oddity.

Price also plays a part. The goal is to educate consumers as to why what you have for sale is a genuinely good value. (Remember when I asked a friend after treating him over the phone how much he'd pay for a similar service?)

This can prove particularly challenging. If yours is a business with a revolutionary or even relatively new product or service, many customers may be hard pressed to identify a "fair" price. Since they've never paid for something akin to what you're offering, they have no perspective.

EDUCATE THE MASSES: HOW TWO COMPANIES DID IT JUST RIGHT

Although the challenge of building consumer understanding will differ from one situation to the next, two real-life cases stand out as effective and systematic examples.

The first is Amazon. Amazon started with just books—remember? I certainly do. I thought it was amazingly cool. You go online, place an order, and your book arrives in a few days' time—quite often, at a lower price than conventional book retailers. Later, of course, that timeline was boiled down to just a minute or two with Kindle immediate downloads.

As an avid reader, I've always loved going to bookstores, but the convenience and immediacy of Amazon struck a chord with me. Before long, ordering a book online from Amazon became completely natural to me.

Obviously I wasn't alone in that reaction. As people increasingly turned to Amazon to buy books, Jeff Bezos gradually and systematically began to expand the company's product lines—appliances, music, food, you name it. Because they had started small and established a psychological basis that allowed shoppers to become comfortable with online shopping, it was natural to add products that customers would associate with Amazon. They were cost effective, convenient and, eventually, a place to find most anything you could imagine.

In effect, Bezos found his target audience in part by building it himself. By starting with an MVP—books—he educated his audience about online shopping's cost effectiveness and convenience.

Here's another example of an iconic company that built its success through a sustainable means of educating customers. When Nick Swinmurn first came up with the idea of Zappos—selling shoes online—he was rejected by every venture capitalist he approached. At the time, so it seemed, no one would ever be comfortable buying shoes online. An in-person setting seemed essential—getting the right size, walking around to see if the shoes were comfortable, and other well-embedded habits.

Investing huge sums of money in what seemed an utterly foreign idea was business suicide. Instead, Swinmurn went low and slow. He went to several shoe stores, took some photographs of inventory, then promised to pay the store full price if he actually sold anything. He built a website and posted the photographs.

The essential idea was not without precedent. When the company was founded in the late 1990s, 5 percent of all shoes sales in the United States were mail order. If that experience could be replicated and improved upon online, consumers would become educated and comfortable buying shoes from somewhere other than catalog or a brick-and-mortar store. There was a definite target audience in view.

This illustrates an entrepreneur leveraging a minimum viable product to build an educated market (more about this shortly.) To further consumer understanding and comfort level, Zappos has solidified a well established reputation for customer service. Purchases and returns are free of shipping charges. The company has also established a simple, effective system that makes sending items back to the company virtually hassle-free.

For me, one essential component of Zappos's successful education of its target market is its generous return time frame—as long as one year after purchase. What better way for consumers to become comfortable than by offering them 365 days to make up their minds?

With Amazon and Zappos, the companies not only identified a target audience but also effectively built one through a carefully orchestrated MVP rollout. By taking things slow and simple, they were able to educate the masses who are the cornerstone of both companies' extraordinary success.

Not every entrepreneur follows that sensible path. There were no other competing urgent care centers when I opened three in the Denver area a number of years ago. Still, urgent care seemed to make sense. The area demographics identified an audience of active, healthy people. If they became sick or injured, they would want to heal quickly and inexpensively. It seemed a no-brainer.

On the day of our grand opening, I remember a gentleman coming up to me, a puzzled look on his face.

"Do I have to be really sick to come to an urgent care?" he asked me. "Do I have to be sicker to come here than to an emergency room?"

Right then I knew I was screwed. This was obviously a well-educated person, but he had no idea what an urgent care facility did. Of course, he was a sample of just one, but I also knew that I would have to spend time and resources educating the market. I had a solution to a problem few knew they had. By accident, I had taken the Steve Jobs approach: "Our job is to figure out what they are going to want before they do."

It was an uphill slog. We had TV commercials, mailers, door hangers, and refrigerator magnets. It's unimaginable that anybody today doesn't understand what an urgent care is, but that was the environment we found ourselves in back then. It was another example of my assuming I had an audience when, in fact, there was none at the time.

HOW TO DEFINE A TARGET AUDIENCE

The first step in defining a target audience carries a caveat. Never think you know for certain that you have a target market without taking steps to make absolutely certain.

That's what happened to me with the Colorado urgent care clinics. I assumed that people would understand the purpose of urgent care clinics. They didn't, and as a result I had to spend a lot of money to educate them.

That makes a proactive effort to identify and understand your target market critical. Everybody has great ideas, but entrepreneurs have the ability to execute those ideas in the real world. In order to do this, you must identify a viable target audience; otherwise there is simply no value. Remember the admonition of Henry Ford: "If I'd asked customers what they wanted, they would have told me, 'A faster horse.'"

Although there are many ways to go about that, start with a complete, understandable definition of precisely what your product or service is. Write down

> Everybody has great ideas, but entrepreneurs have the ability to execute those ideas in the real world.

every aspect and feature. What exactly does it do? How does it do it? For your MVP, this will be a short list. However, your list will grow if your initial assumptions are correct.

For instance, an urgent care clinic is designed to treat common, non-life-threatening illnesses and injuries, such as allergic reactions, cuts, burns, animal bites, and other minor problems. Some facilities may also be able to treat minor fractures.

The "how" focuses on efficiency and speed. The central dynamic is that patients can be seen and treated relatively quickly. That obviously differs from calling up your family doctor and trying to make an appointment or waiting hours at an emergency room. With urgent care, patients are seen, their problem addressed, and they're on their way.

From there, identify the potential benefits of your idea. With urgent care, one obvious benefit is that patients can receive necessary healthcare quickly and conveniently. An additional plus is cost. A patient may pay less for a particular service than they would at an emergency room. Depending on the location, getting to an urgent care facility may be a good deal faster than other, more traditional choices.

Any specialization is an added benefit. Some urgent care clinics focus on pediatrics, making them ideal for parents with a child with a minor health issue. Other clinics specialize in women's health or orthopedics.

From there your next step is simple market research. Solicit feedback and thoughts from a variety of people. If this service were available, would you use it? If so, for what price? Instead of going to your family doctor for minor issues, what would it take for you to switch to an urgent care clinic? How far would you be willing to travel?

Be certain to talk to all sorts of people, not just those who are like you. You're going to want to hear both positives and negatives. Constructive criticism isn't a reason to completely abandon the idea. Rather, you may need to adjust, for instance, to lower the price for certain services to appeal to a broader array of people.

This legwork can provide other valuable insights. Pay attention to any patterns in the feedback you're getting. Are older people more amenable to higher price points than younger folks? Are there certain populations who are open to specific services but not others? Who's showing the most enthusiasm? Who's showing the least?

Pay attention to demographics. Look for any patterns according to age, gender, income, education, and other characteristics. Is your potential audience primarily married or single? What do they do for a living? What do they do for fun? This can give you a comprehensive idea of your target audience.

This sort of data can suggest how much work may be required to educate your target audience. Are there some people who readily "get" your idea? Conversely, do you find yourself repeatedly explaining your idea at length? That can hint at how much proactive education will be necessary for people to understand your idea.

Don't worry if your research suggests a relatively small target audience. Remember the Pareto Principle: 20 percent of the causes produce 80 percent of the effects. Translated to your business, this means 80 percent of your sales come from a core group of 20 percent of ideal customers. The better you come to know and understand that 20 percent, the better your results. Again, if your solution really solves a problem, it should not be hard to find your target audience.

Of course, there's always the option of paying a professional to help identify a target audience. Outsourcing target audience research can put this essential task into the hands of experienced researchers who can perform more extensive legwork than you may have time for. Research firms also have access to market data and other valuable information, such as demographics, market saturation, and any barriers to getting started in a particular setting. That's the kind of bandwidth many individual entrepreneurs simply don't have.

There are limits. Avoid handing off the task of researching a target audience and then becoming uninvolved. Stay in the loop. Ask to be informed in real time when significant findings are identified. Stay in close contact with your research team. Closely involving yourself in the process will help you to better understand research results.

Outsourcing research is not inexpensive. Just how expensive it is will depend on the nature and scope of the services performed, but it's never cheap. On the other hand, investing in professional research may save you serious money down the line by allowing you to avoid costly mistakes—including judging whether your business idea is solid to begin with.

REMEMBER YOUR MINIMUM VIABLE PRODUCT

Another valuable tool in identifying your target audience is your minimum viable product (MVP).

Our discussion in Chapter Three outlined the value of using an MVP to determine whether your business idea is, in fact, viable. An MVP can also help delineate your target audience. As you accumulate research and insight through the use of an MVP, pay attention to the demographics and other characteristics of the people offering feedback. Does a particular segment of the group respond more positively to your product or service? By contrast, is there another segment that expresses doubts or misgivings? What are the characteristics of each group—is it a matter of age, education, income, or some other parameter that separates supporters from skeptics?

A usable MVP is essential in finding out whether your product or service has lasting value and appeal. Further, it can help you identify those people who are particularly enthusiastic—the target audience on whom you'll wish to focus your attention.

REACHING OUT, AFFORDING
CUSTOMER ACQUISITION

Thanks to all this information, you're beginning to get a clear picture of who your ideal potential audience might be. It's an exciting step in the entrepreneurial journey. You're getting a sense that there may in fact be a substantial core of consumers who have a genuine interest in your product or service.

But there's more research to be done—specifically, how to connect with your target audience in a cost-efficient manner. It's an important consideration—your legwork suggests you may command a real audience, but it may be a great idea that's simply too costly to execute.

One effective way to begin is to ask questions. Talk to people with whom you've shared your idea or who have used your MVP. What would they suggest is the best way to reach out and connect with others who might also have an interest in your business? Consider drawing up a survey to collect customer outreach ideas. Keep it short—it shouldn't take more than a few minutes to complete, but the more people who contribute feedback, the closer you'll move toward actionable information.

Connecting with your target audience will depend in part on demographics—information and data you've already begun to compile and analyze. For instance, a younger audience is more likely to be reached via social media networks such as Facebook and Twitter, while an audience that skews slightly older may be accessible via email or direct mail.

Whatever you do, staying close to your customers is absolutely critical. These early adopters will allow you to determine the functions you add or shelve as you iterate through your MVP.

Consider the role of consumer education in connecting with customers. Needless to say, any outreach will need to show potential customers how your product or service will benefit them, but that's a tough mountain to climb if they don't already understand your product or service.

This analysis can help you zero in on the means to connect with your target audience. If education is in fact an important component of your customer outreach, tools such as blogs, website FAQs, down-loadable e-books, and other vehicles that naturally lend themselves to explaining what you do may be ideal.

An effective strategy to connect with your target audience should always incorporate value. Every bit of communication should ideally offer something the person at the other end can use to their benefit. Focus on "pain points"—what problems might you help solve? For instance, if your target audience is comprised of time-starved professionals, emphasize speed and efficiency. Point out that your telemedicine business is 24-7, the average amount of treatment time is twelve minutes, and that they don't have to leave their home or office.

> An effective strategy to connect with your target audience should always incorporate value. Every bit of communication should ideally offer something the person at the other end can use to their benefit.

This leads to another challenge—the expense of customer acquisition.

What will that cost you, and how can you keep the cost down?

Like many other topics, I learned about this one the hard way. When I started MeMD in 2010, I was spending $70 per patient acquired. Problem was, on average, that patient was spending only $50 on average!

Here a common formula is important to understand—your customer acquisition cost (CAC). The formula involves dividing the total cost of sales, marketing, and other outreach programs by the number of customers acquired. If you spend $36,000 to acquire 1000 patients, your CAC is $36.

What constitutes a "good" CAC varies from one industry to

the next. But as a general rule of thumb, you want your acquisition expenses to be as low as possible.

If that sounds simplistic, that's because it is. A more meaningful and empirical way of gauging acquisition costs involves another formula, this one known as customer lifetime value (CLV). This, as the name implies, calculates the value of a customer throughout his or her entire experience with your business. For instance, let's say you have an urgent care clinic that has seen a patient for three years. If in each of those individual three years, the patients spends $100 a year, that's $300 over three years.

From there, compare the CLV to your customer acquisition through this calculation: CLV divided by CAC. Then apply the following rules to that comparison:

- If CLV divided by CAC is less than one, you're losing money with every new customer.

- If CLV divided by CAC is one, you're just breaking even.

- If CLV divided by CAC is greater than one, you're earning money on every new customer you acquire. It makes sense to spend $20 to get somebody who's spending $50 three times a year. That's a return on investment that we all can definitely live with. That's also why customer service is so critical—once you have a customer on board, do everything to keep them.

Take Blue Apron as an example. The company was started by two entrepreneurs in 2012. In five years it had a market cap of more than $2 billion. But by 2020 the market cap had tumbled to roughly $93 million.

What happened? When they started, they had a massive total available market (TAM) and 40 percent year over year growth. The challenge was that, while their CAC was reportedly $94, the actual cost was much higher (nearly \$460). With an average order value of \$57.50 at 4.4 orders per quarter, it's easy to see that the CAC exceeded their margin on a per customer basis.

Since customers were leaving faster than they could acquire them, the business declined precipitously. Reportedly, only 10 percent of Blue Apron's customers were still using the service by the end of the second year of business.

SELECTING AN OUTREACH STRATEGY

Here's an overview of some of the options you can use to connect with your target audience:

- Marketing via social media. Here you create and post on a social media network such as Facebook or Twitter. Activities include posting text and images, blogs, videos, and other content to drive audience engagement. Paid social media advertising also falls under this heading, including Google ads, ads on Facebook, and other settings.

- Email marketing. With this, email campaigns and "blasts" are sent to a targeted audience. One attractive aspect is that they can be automated, so emails can be preprogrammed to be sent at particular times to particular target clients. Email may be old-school, but it has an extraordinarily high return on investment provided it is done correctly.

- Traditional ads, including mail campaigns, flyers, brochures, radio and television advertising, and other tools. I've mentioned that I've used several of these in the past and I've found them to be both effective and a bit refreshing (these sort of outreach campaigns tend to be overlooked amid a focus on tech-based options.)

- Search engine optimization (SEO). Want to tap into the more than three billion searches performed online every day? Proper search engine optimization (SEO) makes it possible. SEO is simply the process of improving your website content to increase search visibility. When you optimize content, search engines favor your site and rank your page higher than others. The key is "long tail" keywords and phrases that are very specific to whatever you are selling that consumers are searching for. SEO research can also help you discover search terms that consumers use to find competitors' websites. Once you have data mined those websites, you can create more valuable content than your competitors. Additionally, having a higher domain authority (DA)—a score that predicts website search rankings—indicates how well your website will rank on search engine result pages (SERPs). The higher the DA, the easier it is for you to rank toward the top.

Naturally, it's essential to track and evaluate the effectiveness of any outreach campaign. That offers a clear picture of what's working and what's not. Tools such as Google Analytics let you analyze website traffic to gauge how visitors are arriving at your website and what they do once they get there. With email campaigns you'll want to know about open and click-through rates, frequency of mail "bounces," and other data (there are any number of software options that do this). If you advertise via Google Ads, Facebook, and other locations, investigate the average CAC for your industry to see how yours compares (for instance, the CAC for healthcare for Facebook ads is significantly lower than that of Google ads).

However essential, these steps are potentially very expensive. Fortunately, there are other, more affordable strategies:

- Keep building your email lists. Since email's ROI is so solid, it makes sense to leverage it fully. Try to obtain an email from every visitor to your website. The bigger your email list, the less money you may have to spend on paid advertising.

- Emphasize customer retention. Every customer who returns is one you don't have to replace. Acquiring new customers is expensive. To boost retention, consider investing in a customer relationship management (CRM) system to manage customer data and improve customer service. Additionally, look for upsell opportunities—new products and services can help keep customers happy and engaged. For instance, an urgent care center can also offer vitamins, wearable devices, and other health-related products.

- Make certain your website is in top operating form. Visitors bolt from slow, poorly designed websites. Check that your site loads quickly and that it's clear and readable on mobile devices.

- Perform A/B testing. Also known as split testing, A/B testing is a process of comparing two versions of a website, email, or other outreach tool and seeing which performs better. It's something like a focus group—you give one version to one group and the other to a second group and evaluate which does better.

- Encourage referrals with rewards. A reward referral program is one of the most cost-effective strategies to reduce acquisition expenses. Encourage current customers by offering discounts, specials, and other incentives.

This may all seem like a monumental task—one requiring extensive detail and discussion. But that's not necessarily true. You can devise a powerful, comprehensive summation of your business in just one page.

That's right, I said it. A one-page business plan.

CHAPTER FIVE

CRAFT A ONE-PAGE BUSINESS PLAN

Mention a business plan to a first-time entrepreneur and watch the color drain from their face.

By popular reckoning, business plans are very long, exceedingly detailed, and for many, a terrifying writing challenge.

Much of that is true. Business plans can be long and comprehensive. Moreover, they can command a fair amount of time and research to piece together—often a problematic amount of time, particularly for time-strapped physicians.

I have written my share of business plans over the years. Most were forty to sixty pages long and delved ad nauseam into every possible nuance of the business, the competition, the risks, and the planned exit. They were painful to write and just as time-draining.

Even more frustratingly, their shelf life was limited. As in the saying about war that "All plans are out the window when the enemy is first encountered," most business plans fall apart after the first pivot. Any bit of unanticipated news or change and they're largely obsolete.

But I didn't specifically say that every plan *has* to be lengthy and tiresome to put together. If all you need is a reasonably complete road map for your business, it's often possible to put all that together in a single page.

Don't misunderstand me. A one-page business plan isn't appropriate in all cases. But it is entirely plausible to draft a useful business plan in one page, provided you know what should go into it and how to keep things on point.

BUSINESS PLANS DEFINED (AND THE CASE FOR A ONE-PAGE PLAN)

A business plan is a written document that describes the activities of a business in detail. It provides information about key personnel, as well as target markets and audiences. A well-crafted business plan points out any strengths and challenges the business may face, along with strategies and ideas with which to meet those obstacles.

But a business plan should do more than simply list details. The plan should also serve as a GPS or map used by a driver when traveling to an unfamiliar destination. It's a playbook that specifies turn-by-turn directions, allowing you to navigate the twists and detours of an unpredictable journey.

That runs counter to the argument for a business plan that's lengthy and detailed. If, as often happens, certain elements of a comprehensive plan are out the window once the business encounters marketplace realities, it just doesn't make sense to devote time and resources to something doomed to be obsolete.

That's one of the most compelling reasons for the one-page plan. Here you focus your thoughts and energies on a succinct summation of your business. In fact, you may not spend much less time thinking about a one-page plan than you would its lengthier siblings—not only are you charged with keeping things tight, but you also still have to spend a good deal of time thinking about the same sorts of issues.

One advantage to all types of business plans is that they force you to evaluate every element of your business. A solid plan doesn't let you slough off anything, be that the product or service itself, your target audience and ways to connect with them, or the finances necessary to achieve that.

A one-page plan also allows you to pivot more effectively should that prove necessary. If by chance your idea doesn't pan out initially, you haven't invested time and sweat into a forty-page document that instantly becomes irrelevant.

Approach a one-page plan as you would an elevator pitch—albeit one in a tall building. It's a great tool to help you get your ideas down on paper so that you and your colleagues can start iterating various ideas and strategies. The components of the plan are basically the same as those of a full business plan, but without inordinate discussion and detail. You're simply focusing on the big picture.

I think many entrepreneurs place too much importance on a lengthy, detailed business plan. No one, especially a physician with a litany of responsibilities, has time for forty pages or more. Although one may prove necessary later in the business's life span, it's far better and constructive to put together a one-page plan, devise a minimum viable product, and bring it to the marketplace quickly. That's where the rubber truly meets the road.

THE COMPONENTS OF THE ONE-PAGE PLAN

Now to laying out the elements of the one-page plan. If you've seen other plans before, you'll notice that the contents and the order of the material are similar to those of longer plans. The primary difference is in how succinctly ideas are discussed.

The one-page plan should address:

- **Your Customers**—Just who will be the primary target for your product or service? Leverage the strategies and information we discussed in Chapter Four to offer a clear picture of who should find your idea appealing. Don't be all things to all people.

- **Their Problem**—This is the primary issue or problem that defines your target audience. If you don't have a problem that needs to be addressed, then you don't have a business.

- **Your Solution**—How does your product or solution specifically address that problem? What solves or mitigates the problem experienced by your target audience? Anyone can point out a problem—an entrepreneur devises a solution.

- **Competitors**—Who else is doing what you're doing, or is at least attempting to? What about their product or service is ineffective or insufficient in solving your audience's key problems?

- **What Distinguishes Your Product or Service**—How is your product or service different from others? You should be at least ten times better than your competitors if you are not first to market.

- **The Team**—Identify key members of your company. Point out credentials or relevant experiences that make them valuable.

- **Current Available Resources**—What do you have in terms of resources that are already in place? This can include facilities, financial resources, and other elements.

- **What Resources You'll Need**—Additional financing, facilities, human resources, and other components necessary to further develop the business.

- **Simple Financial Forecast**—This is a stripped-down pre-diction of how you expect the business to perform. This can include sales or revenue forecasts, expenses, assets and liabilities, and a break even analysis. This can also offer an estimation of a "drop dead" date—that point in time when you decide whether to press on or drop completely (or shelve temporarily) the entire idea. Remember the runway concept. Do you have enough cash to get the product to market and enough cash flow to sustain the business, or will you need investors?

AN ACTUAL BUSINESS PLAN

The following is a real-life one-page plan I drew up for a business that never made it to market. As you no doubt know, clostridium difficile is a bacterium that can cause symptoms ranging from diarrhea to life-threatening sepsis. Our idea was designed to address that by offering an early warning system.

- **Customers**—Nursing homes; long-term care centers; hospitals. The device will be sold through large medical suppliers such as McKesson, who will resell it to various customer segments. Alternatively, the device will be leased directly to facilities.

- **The Problem**—Clostridium difficile affects patients in nursing homes, long-term care centers, and hospitals. It's highly contagious and contributes to mortality, higher patient care costs, and transmission of the disease to others since the patient is contagious a few days before symptoms become overt.

- **The Solution**—A wall-mounted, Wi-Fi-enabled chemical sensor that detects the airborne compound secreted by the organism before the patient's symptoms appear.

- **Competitors**—None. The business owns the patent for the process and device.

- **Unique Value Proposition**—The early detection of C. difficile will allow patients to be treated earlier. Staff will also be better prepared by donning PPE before the onset of overt symptoms.

- **The Team**—John Shufeldt and business development team.

- **Current Available Resources**—Fifty units in stock (average unit of $10,000) and $100,000 in cash.

- **What Resources You Will Need**—None at present.

- **Simple Financial Forecast**—The cost per unit is $10,000. Future cost per unit is $4,500 as more devices are offered and production moves overseas. Margin on unit sales is expected to be 100 percent. Leased units will cash flow in month 11 and then contribute $500 per month per unit.

HOW TO KEEP THINGS TIGHT

An old saying has it that it's much easier to write long than short. That's a truth you'll likely encounter as you craft an effective business plan that limits itself to one page.

Here are some tips to help you keep things as streamlined as possible:

- Watch your language. Avoid flowery words. "Utilize" is just "use" after it reached for a thesaurus.

- Keep sentences as short as possible. Not only do they take up less space, but brief sentences are also easier to read and understand.

- Edit, then edit again. Got a particularly long sentence? Try writing it with half the words. If you're up for a real challenge, try halving the word count again.

- Use bullet points whenever possible. Again, short, to the point, and easy for the reader to absorb.

- Graphs and charts can be helpful to summarize key data in a more efficient manner than a written description.

WHEN YOU NEED MORE

The one-page business plan is a great way to start. However, if you hope to take the business to the next level by attracting financing, investors, bank loans, or grants, you're going to need more than just a one-page summary. Anyone with money will want more meat. One possible exception: if your MVP is up and running, your market is growing month over month, and you're hitting your forecasts, the proof will be in the pudding. As a result, a one-pager may suffice.

If you need more depth, the components of a full-blown business plan won't differ significantly from a one-pager. But there needs to be substantially greater detail and analysis. For instance:

- Comprehensive market analysis, including overall size, trends, and other components

- More thorough examination of competitors, including both direct and indirect competition

- Marketing objectives and procedures

- Quality control

- More comprehensive financial analysis, including detailed revenue examination and possible variations in expenses

The good news is there are numerous relevant templates available—many of which are free—that can help guide you through the more intricate discussion that a complete business includes. For instance, SCORE (Service Corps of Retired Executives—www.score. org) offers just such a template, as well as other tools and resources.

Additionally, should you start with a simple one-page plan and find a more comprehensive version necessary later on, you've already got a jump on identifying many of the major themes. You just need greater detail.

BEST OF ALL—IT MAKES YOU THINK

In my experience, a one-page business plan is more than adequate for start-ups. It can offer a succinct, focused overview of your business and what steps you will need to take to keep things moving forward.

Most importantly it compels you to think carefully about the central features and challenges facing your business. It forces you to break individual ideas down and consider them objectively. Further, by writing them down into a plan, you have a valuable tool in place that you can revisit, change, or expand upon as your idea and the marketplace evolve.

Look at it in terms of being a minimum viable business plan—a document that gets you off the starting blocks and into the race.

Now that the business plan is locked down, let's talk about naming your venture and branding.

CHAPTER SIX

NAME AND BRAND YOUR BUSINESS

Naming and branding your new business matters. A lot. And in more ways than you would probably imagine.

When I opened my first urgent care facility in Arizona, it was called Arizona Family Urgent Care. Simple, to the point, and perfectly descriptive. I thought the name was ideal.

Until I happened to walk by a receptionist who was answering a phone call:

"Hi, this is A-FUC," she announced cheerily. "How may I help you?"

"A-FUC?" I asked her after she finished the call.

"Sure," she replied. "Arizona Family Urgent Care. A-FUC."

Clearly, this was a huge oversight on my part! So I hired a naming company to come up with replacement names. They sent me pages and pages of names. Brickstone Urgent Care, Brownstone Urgent Care—everything imaginable. The naming company kept sending me lists with potential names, none of which moved the needle. I was doing a reverse twenty-four hour shift in the ED, so by hour twenty, I was getting a bit bleary-eyed. I kept hoping that the next one would be it. Then it struck me. The name for the urgent care was NextCare.

The significance of your business's name isn't limited to an inadvertently offensive acronym. Your name and other elements associated with it—your trademark, your brand—are at the core of your identity. They tell customers who you are and what you're about—provided you take the time to choose the best name possible and to intertwine other components seamlessly into the message you convey to customers and teammates.

WHY A NAME MATTERS SO MUCH

Finding the right name that conveys meaning to your audience is a challenging task—all the more so now, with fewer internet domains available.

Your business name is the first impression a potential client or customer has of your business. As the old saying goes, you never have a second chance to make a first impression, so make certain you get the first pass right.

Names can achieve all sorts of goals. They can inform. They can elicit emotion. They can entertain. They can attract people or push them away.

But if your business name accomplishes anything, it should be to distinguish you. It should set you apart from competitors. Someone seeing your business name should immediately associate something positive or memorable with it. Something that they'll remember (known colloquially as a "sticky" name).

A solid name can convey the experience a prospective customer expects. If that's your objective, make certain that the message you want to get across will actually be understood.

Here's an example. One name I came up with for an urgent care clinic was Mach One Medical. Even though, as a pilot, I know that means the speed of sound, I mistakenly assumed everyone else would be familiar with the term. I wanted it to represent the speed and focus patients would receive.

I was wrong. I took it to a marketing firm to design an appropriate logo.

> Someone seeing your business name should immediately associate something positive or memorable with it.

"Hey, that's a cool name if you understand what Mach One means, but most people don't know what Mach One means," one of the marketing people said in a meeting.

"Everybody knows what Mach One means," I countered.

We went around the table, and to my surprise most people didn't understand what Mach One meant. Instead, they proposed an alternative, US Careways, which I thought was a great play on words because this was right after US Airways changed its name. So we named the business US Careways, did the logo, the trademark, the brand, the entire package. It failed, but it went down with a good name—much like the *Titanic*.

It was also another step in my ongoing education about not making assumptions—including in choosing a name.

Understand that the name you choose carries implications beyond what it conveys to your target audience. You need to consider legal issues before you start ordering signs and business cards.

Every state has rules about new business names. In general, you can't choose a name that another business is already using. In addition, it's risky to choose a name that might infringe on another business's registered trademark. If you wish to trademark a business name, you'll need to choose one that meets the criteria for trademark protection. A lawyer can explain the rules and help you research options.

Since so many names are already taken by others, many companies choose names that are essentially made up (think Häagen-Dazs, Waze, Google, and Kodak.) In one respect, that makes sense—if a name you like is already taken, why not be a bit creative? If the company is successful, a made-up name can become synonymous with a particular product or service even though the word isn't in any dictionary. On the other hand, a made-up name can be confusing to consumers, particularly in the case of a start-up company. People may have a hard time grasping what it is you do.

A made-up name can also impact your internet presence—specifically, search engine optimization. Any name that's contrived may be difficult to spell, which will affect how easily it can be searched. When considering any name, take SEO into account. Make it easy for people to find you without going to the trouble of typing in various spellings.

Whatever name may appeal to you, don't underestimate the importance of the right name decided early in your business's life span. You can't overstate the value of coming up with a memorable name that signifies what you're trying to achieve and what you're aspiring to accomplish.

HOW TO CHOOSE A NAME

One way I go about choosing a name for a business begins informally.

Often a name just pops into my head (often, for some reason, while I'm in the shower, running, or meditating). No real focused thought as such, just free association. If it sounds good, I take it from there to the next steps.

But that's not always the case. Sometimes I'm more systematic and scripted. For one thing, I always take any potential future growth into account. If the business really takes off, you don't want to have a name that's too limiting or needs to be changed to reflect your success.

In retrospect, that was the case with Arizona Family Urgent Care. Ignoring the fact that the acronym was something you'd hear in a college frat house, I also hoped to expand the business outside Arizona. Not only was the initial name offensive, but it was also inadequate.

Once I have a name in mind, I do an internet search to see if someone else already has it. Sometimes that matters; sometimes it doesn't. Soon after I started NextCare, I discovered a company in the United Arab Emirates also named NextCare that was started around a year after I trademarked NextCare. I emailed the company. The CEO assured me they were just a little business in the UAE and that it would be no big deal to change their name. I believed him.

Of course, they never did, and I didn't press them any further because I didn't have the money to fight with them. To this day, if you Google NextCare, this Middle East company comes up in the search. It really doesn't matter because the two businesses aren't similar, but it's annoying.

Next, I do a trademark search to see if someone else legally owns the name. Do an online search of the US Patent and Trademark Office at USPTO.gov.

Following that, I address the issue of a domain name. Sites such as GoDaddy.com are just one of many online resources you can check out to see what's available.

My personal preference is domains ending in .com, but of course those aren't always available. For instance, we had to settle for a .me domain for MeMD, the virtual medicine business. Occasionally, someone will appear and try to sell me the .com URL for about $2 million.

Next, I do some legwork regarding legal matters. Since you'll likely choose to form your business as a corporation or an LLC, check with the secretary of state in your state to make sure your name isn't too close to an existing business. If it's too similar, the secretary of state may not allow you to register it.

Your corporate lawyer can help you conduct this kind of search, as well as guide you through all necessary steps to secure the name of your business. If you have any reservations about doing this legwork yourself, delegate it to a professional with much more experience.

Before devoting energy and resources to securing a business name, share it with as many people as possible—friends, family, colleagues. Once again, seek out people who are different from you and less prone to support the name out of friendship. In particular, ask them what the name conveys about the company, what impression they get.

A more formal approach is to hire a marketing firm. They may recommend a focus group approach for gauging your proposed name—bringing people together, ideally people from your target audience, to solicit feedback and opinions within a more structured, analytic framework. This research will cost you some money, but it's far better to invest in getting the name right from the start rather than having to pivot later on.

Lastly, make certain that you love the name. You're going to be spending a lot of time talking about it and working with it, so be sure that it's a name you enjoy and look forward to growing with.

Even though I've had many businesses over the years, NextCare stands out as my single favorite name. I like it because I think it really embodied the next iteration in healthcare. Maybe a close second is a business called HealthyBid, which allowed patients to solicit bids for certain types of medical procedures, such as elective surgery. I thought that was a great name, although the concept was ahead of its time and the company eventually failed.

For reasons already discussed, Arizona Family Urgent Care (Dead TV was a close second) was probably the worst name I came up with. Although the name described exactly what we were, it was boring, unimaginative, and the acronym funny but offensive. Not far behind in the dud category is a 501(c)(3) not-for-profit concept show I thought up called *Dancing with the Disabled*. I thought it was a unique way to raise money for physically challenged people while also highlighting their daily struggles. Everyone I ran the concept by said, "You're joking, right?"

PROTECTING YOUR NAME AND YOUR BUSINESS

Once you have a name in place that you like, you'll also develop accompanying materials, such as a logo, packaging, and other items that showcase the name.

It's essential that they all are adequately protected.

Let's begin with trademarks. Trademarks can be used to identify the business and distinguish it from others. A trademark can be a word, phrase, symbol, or design. Similarly, a service mark distinguishes the source of a service rather than goods. Although they are technically different, people often refer to trademarks as protecting both goods and services.

Trademark registration isn't an absolute must. You can establish "common law" rights based just on your use of the mark. However, trademark registration with the federal government carries significant advantages—a notice to the public of the registrant's claim of ownership of the mark, a legal presumption of nationwide ownership, and the exclusive right to use the name.

Registering a trademark for a company name is fairly simple. Many business owners can complete an application in a couple of hours without having an attorney. Begin by going to the US Patent and Trademark Office's website, www.uspto.gov. First, go through the system's Trademark Electronic Search System database—also known as TESS—to see if another company has registered an identical or even similar name for the same sort of business. It's first come, first served. If someone else has already trademarked your mark, consult your attorney. You might be able to still obtain the trademark, but the process is more involved and expensive.

But if you're first in line, you can file an application. You'll need to supply information such as the categories of goods and services associated with the mark that will be used, when it was first used or will be used, and if there's any sort of design associated with the mark. Cost is between $275 and $325. You should receive a decision within a few months. Federal trademarks are in force for ten years and can be renewed in ten-year increments.

If you're registering an internet-based business, it's best not to include the extension. If you do, businesses can register the very same name, only with a different extension. It's far more important to protect the name itself.

You can always hand off trademark registration to your attorney. In some cases, an attorney is essential, such as when you are dealing with a similar existing trademark. That could mean a legal challenge to your application, something that mandates your attorney's involvement.

Businesses may also seek formal copyright protection for any original material, such as photographs, brochures, and websites. You don't have to register your work to be copyrighted—that happens when the work is first created. However, a formal registration at the federal level establishes a public record of the copyright claim. It's also required for any suit filed against someone you believe is infringing on your copyright.

Lastly, you can pursue patent protection for any sort of invention associated with your business (such as my vibrating tampon idea). Here, there's no do-it-yourself option. It's essential to involve an experienced patent attorney.

DEVELOPING YOUR BRAND

Your business's name, logo, and anything else associated with your business can be boiled down to one component: your brand.

To me, brand means what people think of when they see your logo or your name. What does it convey? What do you stand for? What are the goals you're trying to achieve with your business?

Here's an example. You remember there was a cyanide scare in the 1980s involving the pain reliever Tylenol. The company pulled every last bottle of the product off the shelves all across the world. It cost them $100 million.

You would have assumed the company was ruined. It was anything but. A year later Tylenol was back on the shelves and had regained most of its market share.

The key to that rebirth was the company's focus on the brand of "trust." Rather than associating the product with something deadly, consumers looked at Tylenol with complete trust. Tylenol had recognized that consumers were justifiably frightened. Not only did the company make their packaging completely safe, but they also conveyed that core message to the marketplace. You could trust Tylenol, and the public did just that.

That's branding—a powerful, visceral response to a product or service.

There are countless others. With Apple, when you see fruit with a bite missing, you think "reliable." When you see a Volvo on the street, you associate it with safety. And when consumers see or think of your business, you want to elicit a similarly positive response. As Amazon's Jeff Bezos once put it, "A brand is something someone says about your company when you're not around to hear it."

Start to build your brand by asking one central question: What are you trying to achieve? What's your genuine purpose? For instance, an urgent care center can offer all sorts of medical services and treatments, but what is the underlying dynamic? Quality? Efficiency? Affordability? Those and other attributes are the stuff brands are made of.

Identifying your brand may involve a little cerebral digging on your part to go beyond your business's rudimentary elements. What is your overriding mission and vision?

One useful example is the tribal emergency medicine business—Tribal EM—that I'm involved with. Our goal is to provide exceptional care to Native Americans, a demographic that is sorely in need of quality healthcare. Due in large part to two hundred years of purposeful disenfranchisement, Native Americans have a life expectancy that's at least five years less than that of the average American. They die at higher rates than other Americans due to many health issues, including chronic liver disease, cirrhosis, diabetes, suicide, and chronic respiratory diseases, just to cite a few.[3]

There's also a pattern of generational trauma. Native Americans have come to expect these sorts of challenges; the associated trauma is

---

3   Indian Health Services, 2020. "Disparities," https://www.ihs.gov/newsroom/factsheets/disparities.

passed down from one generation to the next. It's absolutely appalling that anyone, let alone the people who are the original inhabitants of this country, are treated so poorly. The purpose of Tribal EM is to change that.

Part of our brand is to counter the expectation of poor-quality care that was pervasive for years on tribal lands. We want to have an impact when a mother brings her child to one of the emergency departments or clinics we staff and receives great service. She thinks, *Wow, maybe these people…maybe they actually do care.* And then she goes and tells her family, friends, and other members of the community. We believe that's how we can help make generational changes to ease the trauma that indigenous people carry.

That's our brand. Our vision and values are embodied in making generational impact through outstanding patient care—maybe for the first time in the patients' lives.

Consider your target audience when weighing a brand. Based on what you know about your designated market, does your brand resonate with their values and priorities? What does it make them think or feel? Does your brand signify a solution to a problem?

The next step in brand development is making sure that your brand message is consistent across everything in your business. For instance, in every one of our monthly Tribal EM newsletters, we talk about taking care of each other and our patients. That message is also a prominent part of our website. Everything that you convey to a

> Consider your target audience when weighing a brand. Based on what you know about your designated market, does your brand resonate with their values and priorities?

customer segues or ties back into that brand. There should be absolutely no exceptions.

There's also an internal value to consistent branding. Tribal EM nearly lost its contract to service Native American reservations due to a legal loophole a competitor took advantage of. We solved the issue and kept the contract, in large part because everyone on our team stuck together because of their belief in our brand. Your employees should live the importance of your brand so that customers experience your values by your employees' actions. Focus on clear continuity to your messaging, your actions, your public statements, and any communication with your team.

Another step toward a powerful brand is to investigate whether you're inadvertently sending the wrong sort of message. For instance, if your urgent care center's brand is speed of care, you don't want to convey the impression that patients are rushed through on a conveyor belt. In that instance, you'll want to review all materials that may even hint at needless speed and instead reinforce the message of thoughtful care coupled with efficiency.

There are other ways to guard against this. A focus group sort of format can be helpful not only in pinpointing what your brand conveys to others but also if what's meant to be positive can be misinterpreted. Additionally, try to imagine just how your target audience might misread your message. Be as twisted and unfettered in your thinking as possible—you want to consider every conceivable possible misinterpretation, including ones that defy every scrap of logic.

Consider the long term as well. Ask yourself if your branding message will come back to bite you (for instance, if you shift product lines significantly or change your business's core function). Further, will the brand hold up over time and be as relevant as it was in the early stages of your business?

Building a brand—including a name, logo, and all products, services, or materials associated with your business—is critical to gaining a solid foothold in the marketplace. Protect your brand and be 100 percent consistent in your use of it. It's much more than a mere label.

Next up—the numbers behind the finances of your business.

CHAPTER SEVEN

MONEY MATTERS

I f you've become accustomed to the comfort of a regular paycheck, bear this story in mind.

When I started NextCare, I didn't pay myself, even when I was covering a shift, for the first seven years.

That's a long time to go without a paycheck. I had to continue to work full-time in the ED to make ends meet. In retrospect, it was somewhat unnecessary. Granted, I started the company with very little money in the bank, but I could have easily paid myself something. (Side note—you should pay yourself at least minimum wage when you start a business, particularly if the business is in California.)

I mention that anecdote for several reasons. For one thing, folks new to start-ups and building a business need to understand that being an entrepreneur involves sacrifice. That's not just in time and resources, but also in terms of financial priorities.

There's an old saying about starting a business—leaders eat last. That's very true. Founders often have to be comfortable being seated at the end of the line. A lot of things can come before their getting paid.

At one point during a particularly dire cash flow period, I had to sell a helicopter I owned to meet payroll. Our house was triple mortgaged, and I was simply out of cash. I bought the copter for $150,000 and sold it for $225,000. The cash from the sale gave me enough to survive until I was able to secure another bank loan. Although a helicopter sounds like an extravagance, it saved me about ninety minutes per day of travel time. Watching it fly away was bittersweet to say the least.

That illustrates the sacrifices many entrepreneurs have to make to do whatever is possible to build their business. But that story also shows that an entrepreneur needs to be closely involved with the finances of their business. It was also about this time that I learned that a trusted employee had embezzled more than $70,000. As my helicopter and embezzlement anecdote shows, your finances will always manage to find you. Far better you find them first.

That calls for more than just a rudimentary understanding of your business's finances. This is one issue that founders and entrepreneurs have to have their heads around right out of the gate. They need a real understanding of what's going on. They have to manage their money in as hands-on and proactive a way as possible. I was shocked how easy it was for someone with access to the books to steal from right under my nose.

This runs somewhat counter to some of the other topics I've covered to this point. For instance, with legal matters, it's only common sense to defer to your attorney. You'll want to know what your attorney does and why, but your understanding doesn't have to be encyclopedic.

Not quite so with your money. True, you have a bookkeeper to track accounts and handle payments and a CPA to guide you on tax matters, but the day-to-day finances of your business are different.

You can begin your entrepreneurial journey with a rudimentary grasp of money matters, but you'll need to learn more over time. Your business's finances are your lifeblood.

BOOKKEEPING 101

In a way bookkeeping mirrors a business's evolution. As a company grows and becomes more complicated, so too does the need for more detailed record keeping. That dictates, to some degree, who should be performing the actual bookkeeping. In the early days, you're likely more than qualified to follow the coming and going of your money. As things become more involved, outsourcing or hiring an internal accountant or bookkeeper makes more sense. In the earliest stages of your business, financial matters are often straightforward. Still, where do you start?

You probably already have a better grasp of this than you might give yourself credit for. For example, start with the balance sheet that details your business's assets and liabilities. Next, a profit and loss summary is an overall summary of your revenue and expenses. Third, a cash flow statement examines how your money's coming in and where it's going.

Work with your accountant to set up an online financial accounting system like QuickBooks. This gives you the ability to maintain comprehensive financial records with your accountant's oversight.

But even when you are a new entrepreneur, it's valuable to move beyond these numbers and learn how to interpret the more meaningful data they can offer.

Let's start with some basics, beginning with your bank account.

How much money do you have in your account? You can get this from your online statement. Don't treat it as a static number. It's essential that you understand just how long that money is going to last. That's where we get into your burn rate.

As the name implies, that refers to how long the money in your account is going to last. Employ a simple formula—divide the balance by the amount of money you spend, in this case monthly. How much is going out in expenses, payroll, and other regular expenses? For instance, with $200,000 in the bank and $20,000 in monthly expenses (burn rate), that comes to ten months—known as the runway or the amount of time supported by the finances on hand.

Obviously, your expenses will either rise or fall from month to month. To take that into account, calculate a longer-term average, such as six months. That reflects the ebb and flow of your costs.

Additionally, consider what revenue you bring in every month by adding it to whatever ready cash you have. That will give you the most accurate month-to-month picture, which, in turn, will allow you to determine your runway.

Ideally, you're looking for a runway that's at least one year long. Anything short of twelve months means your financing and revenue may not be substantial enough to keep the business going long enough to become profitable. Moreover, you'll have less leverage when trying to attract investors.

The calculations that identify the length of your runway are essential. To use a medical term, it delineates whether you're alive or on a DNR order. If you're alive, you've got enough money to move toward profitability or additional fundraising. But if you fall into the DNR category, you're not going to reach profitability and won't have much leverage to negotiate financing—more about this later in the chapter.

Another thing you need to calculate is your growth rate. Your investors will want to see a significant month-to-month growth rate.

Calculating growth involves comparing revenue from one month to the next. For instance, if in one month revenue amounts to $10,000 and grows to $12,000 the following month, divide the difference ($2,000) by the initial amount, $10,000. That comes to a growth rate of 20 percent per month.

If your business continues to grow at a 20 percent growth rate month after month, it produces the growth pattern (the hockey stick shape) that knowledgeable investors look for.

Frequently, it can take a while to reach the growth that every entrepreneur wants. For instance, in the urgent care world, it took between nine and twelve months for clinics to reach "cash flow break even"—when income and expenses are roughly equal and you're on the verge of becoming profitable. In my company's case, that was equal to roughly twenty-eight patients per day. (In my virtual medicine business, that time period was much longer. But, in the private autopsy business, we hit that mark the first month.)

Frankly, I didn't know any of that when we opened the first urgent care center. But as we grew, it got to be pretty consistent. On average, by month nine we were hitting twenty-eight patients a day with a net collected revenue of about $118 per patient—equal to roughly $100,000 in revenue per month. We knew our burn rate, so it was pretty easy to calculate our runway.

Those sorts of calculations allow you to evaluate your options. You either have enough revenue and cash in the bank to make cash flow break even or you need to start raising capital or securing debt.

High level calculations can keep you from doing what so many entrepreneurs do when their numbers are struggling—throw money at the problem. For instance, when sales are lagging, an entrepreneur may decide to invest in additional salespeople. While that could help, one thing that's certain is additional costs in the form of extra salaries and expenses.

What they often overlook is asking why the product isn't selling. Is it lack of salespeople, or (more likely) is it my product or lack of product market fit?

That can prompt a more thoughtful approach. Instead of hiring more salespeople, evaluate your product market fit. Talk to people using the product. Don't expect them to say the product is great, that you shouldn't change a thing. That never happens. Listen to their suggestions about what to add or change to improve the product.

Based upon their suggestions, consider allocating additional resources to make the product more functional and a better market fit. Depending on your runway, you may be able to do that without additional capital. If your runway is twelve months or longer, you stand a chance of introducing a more viable product. But if you're staring down the barrel of anything short of a year, you're going to need additional funding—fast.

DETERMINING FUNDING NEEDS

Eventually, most businesses need to investigate additional sources of funding. But before that it's critical to determine how much money you're going to need—and when.

The easiest way is by calculating your runway. For instance, if your burn rate is $25,000 a month and you have $75,000 in the bank, and you have a monthly revenue of $10,000 and you predict that you'll need ten months to become financially self-sustaining, you're going to need an additional $75,000.

That's the simple way to do it. But the one thing you don't want is to hit month number nine and realize that an additional $75,000 wasn't sufficient.

That's why it's always prudent to obtain more money than you need. I generally suggest that entrepreneurs obtain an additional six months of funding above and beyond their actual needs. These calculations are part of what is known as a pro forma financial model.

CRAFTING AN "ACCURATE" PRO FORMA

As physicians, we're all acquainted with Latin phrases and expressions. Add pro forma to your repertoire.

A Latin term that means "for the sake of form," pro forma refers to a financial statement based on certain assumptions and projections. In addition to other uses, entrepreneurs and business owners employ pro formas when they need capital. Pro formas can be drafted as full-year pro forma projections that incorporate year-to-date results as well as investment pro forma projections that show how company results will change with additional financial backing. This lets prospective investors evaluate sources and uses of capital and to calculate their investment return.

Anyone with money, such as a bank or other type of investor, will want to review a pro forma—even though it's common knowledge that a pro forma is only a gross analysis and is rarely accurate.

Every entrepreneur in history has declared that his or her numbers are "really conservative." I've taken that expression out of my lexicon because:

1. They're not.

2. No one believes you when you say it anyway.

Still, pro formas remain a quasi-fictional necessity for those seeking funding. When done well, they can prove a valuable planning tool. Further, there are ways to make them as effective and credible as possible.

One is to present several scenarios:

- Best-case scenario: "I'm going to grow 20 percent faster than

I expected."

- Worst-case scenario: "I'm going to grow 30 percent slower than I expected."

- Reasonable scenario: "Here's what I think is going to happen."

Each of those options involve the same basic steps:

1. Calculate revenue projections. Use realistic market assumptions as well as whatever data you've accumulated to date. Talk to other business owners, bankers, and anyone else with relevant experience to gain a sense of a reasonable annual revenue stream.

2. Estimate total liabilities and costs. Liabilities refer to any loans, trade credit, accounts payable, and lines of credit. Costs include leases, employee pay, insurance, licenses, and other expenses. Not only do costs and liabilities show investors what you're paying out, they also present a chance for review to determine if there's any way to lower them.

3. Estimate cash flows. This projects future net income and any asset sales.

4. Draw up account charts. This is an ongoing tracking of expenses and income for reporting and analysis.

Bear in mind the pro forma's purpose—to attract capital or secure debt funding. So, it never hurts to be a bit pie in the sky when presenting your situation. Anyone considering your numbers is likely to discount them anyway, so start a little high.

But don't go overboard. Take a cautiously optimistic approach. If you don't hit your numbers out of the gate or the first quarter goes by and you're drastically below your numbers, you will quickly lose credibility with investors—both current and prospective. It is better to underpromise and overdeliver, especially right out of the gate.

Moreover, missing your initial numbers can have a lingering aftereffect. Once you miss, say, the first quarter, it's hard to catch up. You're constantly trying to dig out of a hole—something that any potential investors are certain to notice.

RAISING MONEY

Fortunately, there are any number of ways (debt, factoring, convertible debt, equity) from which you can obtain capital for your business.

One of the simplest ways to pursue funding goes by the acronym SAFE. A SAFE stands for a simple agreement for future equity. A SAFE allows an investor to invest in a company in exchange for the right to purchase stock in the future when the company decides to raise additional funds.

A SAFE is basically a preliminary round that precedes more involved fundraising. In that regard, it's ideal for start-ups and other early-stage businesses. There are really only two things to negotiate with a SAFE: how much money the investor will put in and at what valuation cap (what the business is worth).

With a SAFE you present an investor with basic facts regarding your business. You detail your MVP and feedback from early users of your product or service, as well as initial and pro forma financials. You promise any investors that they will receive the per share price of the offering—ideally, greater than the price per share of what the investor initially invested. You're effectively rewarding those investors for their confidence in you and your idea.

For example, if you have a $5 million pre–money valuation and investors contribute an additional $1 million, then the post–money valuation of the company is $6 million. The investors then own 16.67 percent of the company.

So-called "angels" often participate in SAFE funding. Angels come by their name honestly. These are generally friends, family, and acquaintances who believe in your concept and who want in on the ground floor. There are also angel groups that look cooperatively for investment opportunities. These occasionally will agree to invest in the SAFE stage of funding.

SAFEs are a simple alternative to what is known as a convertible note. Similar to a SAFE, a convertible note converts into equity. Unlike a SAFE, convertible notes are a form of debt with interest payments and a maturity date.

The other primary difference between a SAFE and a convertible note is one of obligation should your company fail. If that happens, you may remain tied to the convertible note. Since it's a type of debt, you still owe your investors any money they put into your company. With a SAFE, the business owner is personally off the hook for the capital invested.

THAT FOUR LETTER WORD: DEBT

Another way to obtain capital is traditional debt. Used properly, debt can be an integral tool in helping your business grow. The key is understanding how debt can be used positively—knowing the difference between debt that can kick-start growth and debt that can hinder your business.

Start by considering what any debt is going to offer your business. There's debt that can be used to cover short-term funding needs, such as payroll, if you don't have a helicopter to pawn off. Debt can also be leveraged to help proactively build your business, allowing you to invest in personnel, facilities, and infrastructure.

Debt effectively lets you keep complete ownership and control of your business. Choices such as a SAFEs and convertible notes ultimately put a portion of ownership in someone else's hands.

For instance, when I started the urgent care business, I invested my own capital, as did another investor. Eventually, we went out to a bank and borrowed money.

In many ways borrowing from a bank is a test of your resolve. When you borrow from a bank, they will want you to sign a personal guarantee even if you are borrowing through your LLC or C corporation. They'll want to see what sort of income and assets you have should the business fail. Although you have some protection against creditors, it's your name that's attached to the money borrowed, so you're ultimately on the hook for it. Not until you get quite a bit larger will they waive the personal guarantee.

Given their income level, most physicians will likely have little problem obtaining a bank loan. But it's nonetheless something of a watershed event for your business. Do you truly believe that what you're trying to achieve is solid enough to pledge the equity you have in your home, bank accounts, stocks, and other assets against the loan?

If what a bank offers seems insufficient, it may be possible to leverage additional funds through what is known as factoring. This is tied to receivables—money that is owed your business. This allows you to access funds based on money that is technically yours but that you have yet to receive.

I've done that. For example, in the very early stages of my urgent care business, it often took as long as six months to receive payments from health plans. We couldn't wait that long because we were growing and needed more cash.

We approached a receivables factoring company that specialized in healthcare. The first step is proving your receivables. In our case, we documented funds owed us by the government, health plans, and other sources (they generally won't factor money owed by individual patients). In return, they allowed us to borrow up to the equivalent of 70 to 80 percent of our receivables less than ninety days old.

This is akin to a home equity line of credit—money that's available should you need it. It's a highly fluid option, as the borrowing balance changes literally every day. If in one particular situation, you're owed $1 million, you may be able to borrow $800,000 or 80 percent of receivables on that particular day. If receivables go up, more money is made available; should receivables drop, so too does the amount you can borrow. You'll also get a call that you are overleveraged and will need to pay down the line.

None of this is free. Factoring fees can be as high as 2 to 3 percent for thirty days, although the more receivables you factor, the less the fees are likely to be. How long it takes you to repay the debt—which depends on how long you have to wait to collect receivables due you—also impacts your cost. The shorter the length of the loan, the lower the cost.

Debt often boils down to your level of belief in yourself and your business. How far are you willing to go into debt to afford the best chance possible for success? Consider if that confidence is solid enough to borrow against your own personal credit—your home and other assets. When it comes to debt, it's critical to weigh your financial needs versus your belief in your idea.

It's also essential to have a plan in place to use the money made available to you. Needless to say, it's not prudent to enter into debt without a specific goal or need. Consider:

- How much money are you considering borrowing?

- What are the interest rate and any other associated expenses?

- What's your plan to spend the funds?

- Have you identified a return on investment associated with the money obtained through debt?

- How long do you have to pay back what you borrow? Does the targeted timeline for your expected ROI make repayment manageable and affordable?

- What assets have you tied up as collateral?

SBA LOANS

Small Business Administration (SBA) loans—also known as the 7(a) Loan Program—are one of the most common funding vehicles for start-up businesses. The SBA itself doesn't loan you the money. Instead, it pledges to guarantee a portion of the loan to a lender—usually a bank, community development group, or another lending institution, covering anywhere from 75 to 85 percent of total loan value.

That's one of the SBA loan's most appealing features. Since a government agency will go to bat for you, financially speaking, entrepreneurs with questionable financials may be able to obtain necessary financing.

Additionally, SBA loans generally carry lower interest rates and manageable payback programs (up to twenty-five years for real estate, ten years for equipment, and seven years for working capital).

Now, the caveats. First, there are fees involved—usually a couple of percentage points of the overall loan. Additionally, paperwork necessary to apply for an SBA loan is a long, painful process.

Still, the common belief is SBA loans are entrepreneur friendly. They are to some extent. But you're still approaching a bank or other lending institution. All the SBA is doing is guaranteeing a portion of the loan.

That can backfire. First, the involvement of the SBA isn't necessarily a panacea. If a business applies for a loan with poor financials, the SBA's involvement may make little difference. Bad books are bad books.

Additionally, in some banks' eyes, the fact that the applicant is even considering an SBA loan makes the deal all the riskier: "How many places turned you down before you had to resort to this?"

Additionally, the SBA's pledge to back loans can prove less than advertised. A man and his girlfriend obtained a $300,000 SBA loan to open a beauty shop. A close friend of mine owned the bank that approved the loan. Although they got the loan, the couple later broke up, and the now ex-girlfriend defaulted on the loan.

The bank went to the SBA to recover a share of the loan. The SBA refused. My friend argued the SBA had agreed via email to back the loan with specific provisions met by the now ex-couple who had taken out the loan.

The SBA's response: The person who approved that provision wasn't empowered to do so. He's been fired. Sorry.

Does this make SBA loans awful? No, not at all. For many entrepreneurs, they're valuable lifelines. My point is not to imbue SBA loans with more value than they genuinely offer. They're far from a cure-all for cash-starved start-ups. I have used them in the past, and they work. However, the process is arduous and painful.

VCS AND PRIVATE EQUITY COMPANIES

Your business idea is gaining traction. You've considered funding from angels, bank loans, and others. Maybe you've had a successful funding round using SAFEs. Now is the time to consider other alternatives.

A venture capitalist is an early-stage investor—often a limited partnership of individual investors, as well as insurance companies, pension funds, and university endowments—that deals exclusively in equity. VCs are constantly on the lookout for start-ups with outstanding potential. VCs are also interested in funding later-stage businesses hoping to expand or boost market share.

One intriguing aspect to VCs is that they're often willing to put their money behind companies very early. In some cases, you may not even need a minimum viable product, let alone a record of growth. Instead, VCs are often intrigued by entrepreneurs with a great idea, a target audience, a compelling product or solution, and a clear path to profitability.

Here's why. Given that they often invest in a business at a relatively early stage—and the riskiest stage—VCs are looking for enormous returns. One of the metrics I've heard is that for every ten investments, they expect to hit just one home run. That may seem a poor average, but that one home run is way out of the park—VCs want ten-times-plus return on their money over five to seven years or an average yearly return of 25 percent.

> VCs are often intrigued by entrepreneurs with a great idea, a target audience, a compelling product or solution, and a clear path to profitability.

Another plus is that VCs are very founder-friendly. Unlike other funding sources, they generally want to maintain relationships with the founders. Still, expect a certain amount of involvement in your company (for instance, they will request a seat on a board of directors). VCs inevitably look to stay close to their money.

Venture funds are not long-term. The idea is to invest in a company until it reaches a sufficient scale for sale or a public stock offering.

Entrepreneurs can locate suitable VCs through an introduction, often via another entrepreneur who has given the VC solid leads in the past. If one expresses interest, you'll generally have to submit a formal funding presentation (also known as a pitch deck).

Face-to-face meetings with a VC—involving individual managers and partners—are more than just an examination of the business. You'll want a VC with whom you get along and whose interests and goals align with yours. Consider other forms of value from a VC, including introductions, insight, knowledge of an industry or sector, and other opportunities.

Following presentation of a VC's terms (via a letter of intent), the VC will then perform its due diligence, including a valuation of your company, interviews with staff members, and other forms of research that can take several months. If everything's OK, the VC will fund the business.

VCs can be a tough nut. Estimates hold that the average VC will invest in only a few companies out of a thousand. That means you'll need a solid pitch deck and presentation to attract interest. For more information on how VCs work, as well as guidance for the funding process, consult the National Venture Capital Association at https://nvca.org/.

The next step up is a private equity firm. These are geared to later-stage businesses that have a proven record of profitability and growth. They invest in outcomes that are more predictable.

Additionally, while VCs are founder-friendly, private equity takes a different tack. They generally buy majority ownership of the companies in which they invest, affording them near total control.

As a rule, the company founder usually doesn't survive the private equity transition for more than eighteen months. In fact, once I obtained private equity funding for NextCare, I managed to last two years—a genuine outlier.

NEGOTIATION TIPS

As you can tell, obtaining money from VCs, private equity, and other sources can be daunting. It pays to understand the best ways to approach them.

Start by targeting VCs that have previously invested in your industry. Not only are they familiar with your product or service from an investment standpoint, but they may also be able to offer you specialized help and guidance.

Contact a number of VCs during your search. If more than one expresses interest, you may be able to play off one against another, improving your chances for success and more favorable terms.

Consider your timing. By pursuing VC funding long before you actually need it—a runway of one year and even longer—you offer interested VCs adequate time for due diligence, as well as sufficient time for you to make the best overall pitch. Try to approach them in the wake of positive news, such as a solid quarter. Timely leverage can spur interest.

Lastly, pinpoint the valuation of your company, including the amount of money you wish to raise. That gives VCs an idea of what the company's finances will look like after funding (post–money valuation).

Again, private equity is different. While VCs are accustomed to being approached by founders, it's prudent to hire an investment banker to represent you with private equity companies. They can help you assemble what's called the book or the offering memorandum—a very detailed slide deck about your business, the industry, and your potential for growth. Then they can approach a number of private equity companies.

Whether you're considering a VC or a private equity firm, have at least twelve months of runway in your bank account. Anything less and you lose a lot of negotiating power—as you burn through capital, you lose leverage, increasing the chances of a subpar offer. In their eyes, you really need them. But with eighteen months of runway, you can be more aggressive and selective.

The more the competition, the better. The few times I've been involved with private equity firms, I sent a pitch deck out to more than one hundred firms. We talked with many of them. Many weren't interested, while others said our financials didn't match their parameters.

Eventually, we whittled the list down to ten. After more back and forth, we settled on three that offered the best terms. Finally, we selected one and started the due diligence process. Still, there was a lot of ongoing negotiation, as the private equity firm tried to reduce our valuation.

Ultimately, we got our money on solid terms, thanks in large part to the transaction's competitive nature and an experienced investment banker.

HOW TO TREAT INVESTORS

You may think your work is done when the funds land in your bank account. Truth is, you're just starting the real work.

I've been an investor in a number of companies where once you've invested, you never hear from them again—almost literally, save for the correspondence that they're required by law to send. It's as though they're openly acknowledging that all you are to them is a source of capital.

Don't take that approach. First, it's wrong. Since these are people who believe in what you're doing, you owe them more than just yearly financial disclosures.

By keeping investors informed and up-to-date, you continue to engage them. That can help should you ever need another infusion of funds. A connected investor is far more likely to write a check than one who's out of the loop.

Additionally, investors can offer valuable advice and guidance, particularly to struggling companies. They're more likely to contribute should they feel their input is welcome.

I've always made it a point to remain connected with investors as completely as possible. Our investor agreements specify that at the very least, they'll receive detailed quarterly reports. I've also sent out monthly newsletters. I don't want a single investor to feel as though they have been left in the dark.

It's not just a matter of outreach. I've also started using a platform called Carta, which organizes documents, cap tables, and other pertinent information. An investor can access the system at any time and review ownership structure, their ownership percentage, capitalization figures, and other data. It's another opportunity for connection.

It's not complicated—being transparent with investors and keeping them up to speed is essential. Alternatively, keeping them in the dark will inevitably come back to bite you—if nothing else, investors will quickly put away their checkbooks when you ask them for more money. And, from my point of view, they're justified in feeling frustrated.

> It's not complicated—being transparent with investors and keeping them up to speed is essential. Alternatively, keeping them in the dark will inevitably come back to bite you—if nothing else, investors will quickly put away their checkbooks when you ask them for more money.

INSURANCE AND EQUIPMENT

Since you're a physician, you know the role of insurance. If you're taking care of patients, you absolutely need medical malpractice insurance. That holds true for healthcare-related businesses as well. In general, most physicians purchase "claims made" medical malpractice insurance for one million/three million, which is $1 million coverage per occurrence and $3 million a year. With a "claims made" policy, you need extended reporting endorsement "tail coverage" after exiting the business.

But there are other types of insurance. First is general liability insurance. These policies typically protect you and your company against claims involving bodily injuries and property damage connected to your products, services, or operations.

Another essential insurance is directors and officers (D&O) liability insurance. This protects the personal assets of corporate directors and officers should they be sued for any sort of wrongful act linked to the company. This is as important a type of insurance as any you should have. Many prospective investors will insist that D&O insurance be in place and that they are specifically named in the coverage.

One additional form of coverage that can prove worthwhile is key person insurance. This is a life insurance policy the company buys to protect the lives of top executives. This can prove critical in companies, particularly fast-growing start-ups, where the death or incapacitating illness of the founder or other key personnel would be harmful to the business.

Work with an experienced insurance agent to identify what coverage you need and in what amounts. Any oversight can be devastating.

With regard to whatever equipment your company may need,

my maxim is simple: less is more. It's critical to gauge reaction to your minimum viable product, financial backing, and other issues before investing heavily in new equipment.

For example, in the urgent care world, that means used furniture, a used X-ray machine, and other previously owned items. As much stuff as you can get on a discount, grab it. If you can lease, even better.

It's not forever. At some point you can begin to purchase equipment, but the last thing you want to do is burn cash in the early stages of your business and shorten your runway. Cash burn is always critical.

What's also critical is how you and the people with whom you work see your company. That's a question of company culture and the role everyone plays in crafting a welcoming, engaging environment—the crux of Chapter Eight.

CULTURE, EMPLOYEE RELATIONS, AND LEADERSHIP

I
n many ways, physicians looking to become entrepreneurs have vastly different challenges from others who don't have an MD or DO after their name.

With many start-ups, money is the primary issue. That can certainly be the case with physicians, but it's often not the primary focus. Instead, it can be more an issue of leadership, managing people, and time commitment. To an extent they may have never experienced before, physician-entrepreneurs must lead others.

That can lead to the scourge of micromanaging. Since they've had little experience, physicians who become business owners using their own capital can be understandably tempted to monitor and direct employees' every move.

That's definitely not me. From my perspective, if you hire the right people and give them clearly defined objectives, you don't need to micromanage. Plus, it was the last thing I wanted to do.

But that's a matter of hiring the right people by building the best company culture possible.

CULTURE AS DEFINED BY THE MISSION STATEMENT

There's an old saying that culture eats strategy for breakfast. I think that's very true. If you build an organization with a great culture, it solves a lot of issues proactively. That's because culture helps people do the right thing when there are no rules in place to help them. The company's culture guides them.

I define culture as behavior. It's a "Here's what we're all about" mindset—what we're trying to accomplish, how we hope to accomplish it, and the values and priorities imbued in that journey.

It's crucial you get culture right from the very beginning. As you scale over time, you may not be able to hire every single person. You'll have to rely on the people whom you hired to promote that culture to newcomers. Once you're growing, it's hard to jump back and say, "Let's talk about our culture now." It has to be done early and proactively.

> I define culture as behavior. It's a "Here's what we're all about" mindset—what we're trying to accomplish, how we hope to accomplish it, and the values and priorities imbued in that journey.

It's also empowering. With a defined culture, you're effectively telling everyone in your company that you believe they will do the right thing. Not only does that eliminate the need to micromanage, but it's also inclusive. You trust them to live by the company culture. They're grounded in it because you've hired the right people and inculcated that culture in them.

It's advantageous to have a written summary of your culture, everything your company stands for. That's a mission statement.

A mission statement is a simple, straightforward declaration of your company's goals. It summarizes what you do for your customers, employees, and owners. It explains how you do what you do—and, just as important, why you do it.

A mission statement should be outward-looking. It's what you want to do to change the world, what you do to support customers and teammates.

Here's MeMD's mission statement: "At MeMD, our mission is to provide exceptional care every day, one patient at a time."

A mission statement can also include less serious issues and goals.

Some companies prioritize fun, compassion, energy, or creativity. The overriding goal is to capture your varied priorities in a single statement—one that truly represents what you, your people, and your culture are about.

CULTURE AND THE HIRING PROCESS

Culture and a mission statement aren't standalone entities. They're central not only to how your company and people behave but also to an effective hiring methodology.

I've always made culture as described in our mission statement a central point of hiring. By incorporating culture and values into the recruiting and hiring program, you can identify would-be employees who genuinely embrace those values—the key to obtaining and retaining topflight talent.

An applicant interview is an opportunity to determine how aligned someone is with your company culture. It can be utterly straightforward: "Here's what we're trying to do." Hopefully, the applicant replies, "Yeah, I absolutely want to be a part of that."

For me, alignment with culture is a deal maker and deal breaker—it's that important. If others buy into it—if they expand on your culture in your conversation, identifying elements that have particular value to them—that's an attractive applicant. But if they just don't seem to connect, that's a hard stop. Disconnection from culture will only cause future problems.

Consider using situational questions to identify an applicant's mindset and how closely it matches your company culture:

- "When you had to coach someone else, how did you do it? What was the discussion like?"

- "Give an example when you fired somebody. What was your discussion?"

- "How do you lead by example?"

- "Tell me something you adamantly believe in that most people would disagree with." (Courtesy of entrepreneur and venture capitalist Peter Thiel, this question homes in on how someone thinks.)

The goal is to ask fairly open-ended questions to pinpoint experiences or values that, in the telling, show that the applicant is on board with your culture. In fact, this strategy can be particularly effective since you're not just overtly raising the question of culture. That can avoid the problem of someone simply saying what they think you want to hear. It's far better to approach it unprompted.

Another telling question is also open ended: "How do you improve yourself?" That's particularly important for me. One of the key elements in every company culture I've had a hand in shaping is lifelong learning. Some people will say they listen to podcasts. OK, what podcasts? Others will say they're avid readers. Great—what books?

Of course, you can unexpectedly uncover telling information about an applicant who might otherwise seem attractive. For instance, in one interview I posed the question of recently read books.

"Well, I haven't read a book in a while," came the reply.

"How long is 'a while'?" I asked.

"Since college."

The applicant was roughly forty years old, so I wanted to make sure that I was following the conversation.

"You mean you haven't read a book in twenty years?" I asked, trying to hide how incredulous I felt.

"That's right."

Even though we talked for a while longer, the interview ended right there. He just didn't know it.

There are other strategies to identify cultural alignment. We use predictive indexes extensively in our hiring process. These are behavioral assessments that identify forms of behavior that indicate how a person will think and act in a variety of settings as well as how they see themselves and others.

We also conduct a variety of interviews with several team members. There, among other things, we note how an applicant reacts to different people and personality types. It can be surprisingly telling. We've had applicants who were rude to the executive assistant tasked with coordinating interview times. That was a hard stop—if you can't be kind to everyone on the team, you don't fit our culture.

It's also important that applicants research the company in advance. First, it suggests an interest in every aspect of the company (including culture.) Additionally, it keeps the conversation at a high level, rather than your having to explain every detail. If applicants come to an interview unprepared, it's their last interview.

Ultimately, connection to culture is more important than credentials. By our way of thinking, credentials and expertise are not hard to collect. Behavior and values are other matters entirely. If an applicant doesn't connect with the culture, that carries more weight than somebody having credentials that are off the charts.

It's a straightforward strategy. If you set your mission and vision, define your values, and inculcate both in people, you build a company with team members who don't go astray when there are no specific rules. That establishes the relationship between culture and people. Ultimately, you get the culture right, which ensures you hire right.

One final consideration with new hires: watch how your newcomer leaves their prior employer. That speaks volumes about character and values.

Here's what I mean. I once interviewed someone who seemed attractive as a new hire—that is, until I asked him how soon he could start.

"They've told us they want two weeks' notice, but I can leave right now," he replied.

That was distressing, to say the least. Even if the current employer deserves no notice, that's not what you do. Personally, I never hire somebody who doesn't give adequate notice. I'd rather have somebody say, "I really like those guys. Can I have thirty days? That will give them time to find the right replacement." That's what I want to hear. I never want to hear, "Screw them. I'll leave when I feel like it."

That's always a major red flag. It reveals a lack of personal integrity that's likely to show up again later. And if you hire someone who badmouths their ex-employer, one day he or she will probably bad-mouth you.

WHERE TO FIND EMPLOYEES

This raises the challenge of finding people who are likely solid candidates to join your company.

Our most reliable sources are referrals and word of mouth. Most of our people are friends of friends or colleagues of colleagues. It seems to work well. Someone we know might say, "Hey, I know this person. She certainly personifies the culture of your business, and she's looking for a new job with more upside and that's more aligned with her values. Plus, she's a CPA with great credentials."

Notice the order of information—culture first, then credentials. Culture is our starting point. Job performance comes after that.

We've had some success with advertising. But the best people inevitably come from referrals. Not only do they provide candidates who likely know the company and value culture, but there's also accountability on the person making the referral. No one wants to tout someone who turns out badly.

Of course, there's always the other side of the coin—what about your company attracts well-rounded candidates?

> Culture is our starting point. Job performance comes after that.

There are several ways to approach this. Number one is building a culture in which people want to come to work. They like the atmosphere and feel empowered by it. Number two is how they are treated.

Next, it helps to tie their compensation to success—personal success as well as professional. We meet regularly to address these issues. What are their goals? Going back to school? Advanced professional training? Running a marathon? Specifics aren't always necessary, but you want to serve as a coach and cheerleader to help support them in their pursuit of their goals.

Retaining top performing employees is a matter of emphasizing the same values and priorities that attracted them when they were still just applicants. It's not having a foosball table in the break room or fielding a company softball team. People don't stay because of softball. They stay because they believe in the mission and believe that they're valued and important contributors.

If a company fails to establish and maintain those three core values—mission, a sense of value, and a genuine feeling of working toward something larger than themselves—people start to migrate. If they have a leader who supports and values them, people stay.

CONTRACTS AND OTHER FORMS OF PROTECTION

No matter where you're doing business, you'll be subject to varied laws governing employer-employee relationships. This generally falls under the definition of "at will employment," meaning an employer can fire an employee without any specific reason.

That can make formal employee contracts a dicey proposition. When you are the employer, employee agreements can back you into a corner, as they can run counter to the provisions of at will employment. Since at will employment has been addressed by the Supreme Court, that generally makes employee contracts unnecessary.

One exception involves proprietary information—sensitive and valuable material that you wish to protect. Here it's wise to have every employee sign a confidential information agreement. This stipulates that whatever an employee may be working on under the auspices of the company belongs to that company. This is similar to a non-disclosure agreement but more extensive in nature, as it also protects intellectual property.

Noncompete contracts can also be valuable. Here an employee agrees not to compete with an employer during or after employment.

That includes preventing an employee from leaving your company and starting a competitive firm (potentially using your intellectual property).

It's helpful for business owners to have a working knowledge of contracts, legal compliance, and other similar material. But as with any specialized field, defer to your legal counsel for guidance.

THOUGHTS ON LEADERSHIP

As I mentioned earlier, many physicians will likely find the role of leader a new experience. As such, I can't overstate the importance of acquiring leadership skills.

One way to learn about leadership is seeing how other accomplished leaders have developed effective styles and strategies. I've read a ton about different leaders and different styles. But I don't think you can necessarily mimic an accomplished leader—an "I want to be just like Steve Jobs" approach. That likely won't fly. You can try standing on your desk and yelling at people like Jobs did—but if that's not you, people will immediately see through it. Plus, that's really no way to lead.

Every successful leader displays authenticity. Don't adopt behavior that simply isn't you. Again, people will spot that instantly and they won't recognize you as a genuine leader.

The next step is even harder for many. If you want to lead, set the example. Walk the talk. You can't criticize people who aren't working hard if you're not working hard (or working hard on yourself—a commitment to self-improvement).

A common misconception can hinder understanding of effective leadership. It's not a matter of "Do this, do that." Instead, lead from the front—be the first one in and the last one out. You have to be the hardest worker on the team. To reiterate: leaders eat last.

Leaders who are consistently out in front doing all the hard stuff are known as servant leaders, a term you may know. Servant leaders' primary focus is taking care of the people they lead. What can you do to make their lives better? That goes for professional skills and personal lives. If a servant leader looks after their people, their people will take care of the business and their customers. No barking orders, no bluster—just show that you care.

Great leaders are great communicators. They emphasize simple, clear communication at all times and with everyone. That takes effort and preparation. Communicating clearly can be tough off the cuff. Think carefully about what you're going to say and devote enough to preparation to make certain it's clear, honest, and on point.

President Woodrow Wilson once said it took him a full week to adequately prepare for a ten-minute speech. That's a powerful reminder of what it takes to be a clear and effective communicator— a genuine commitment to own it and do it right.

Additionally, great leaders have to be good judges of people and of character. If you can't read people, all it takes is one bad apple to sink an entire company.

Reading people and their character is a matter of developing empathy and emotional intelligence. As Harper Lee wrote in *To Kill a Mockingbird*, "You never really understand a person until you climb into his skin and walk around in it." I've read that book repeatedly, and that message always resonates. If an employee is challenged by a particular task or project, try to understand how it would feel if that were you. You can see what they're experiencing, which inevitably leads to productive solutions.

A great leader also recognizes what they are not particularly good at. That can take a good deal of personal introspection, as well as simply watching how you perform. For example, I've learned that

I'm good at the start-up phase, but not quite as skilled at being the long-term actual operator. I'm not good at that consistent level of detail. I'm not strong at trying to drive the organization on a daily basis after the first few years. That's why I always try to find others who are really good in the day in, day out environment.

It's also important for an effective leader to admit he or she has made a mistake. A saying goes that a leader takes all the blame and gives out all the praise. That's very true—because the buck stops with you.

It is also more than just words. True, an employee can make a mistake, but it was you, the leader, who hired them. You're ultimately responsible.

The corollary is the quarterback who throws five touchdown passes and immediately credits the five receivers who caught them—as well as the offensive line who gave him time to throw.

Ultimately, a great leader earns the trust of others. They have to trust that you'll take care of them, that you'll take care of the business (and their paychecks). If they're not confident in your ability to provide them gainful, fulfilling employment, little else matters.

One more guideline—praise in public, coach in private. Never reprimand or coach someone in front of others but rather praise the hell out of them in public.

Additionally, when you do have to coach someone, separate the issue from the person. This technique has worked amazingly well for me for many years: "Here is what I need from you. Here is where you are. Let's figure out what we can do to get your performance up to the level that I know you can achieve. I will help and be your biggest cheerleader. Ultimately, however, your performance has to improve for you to remain on the team." If you don't hold everyone to the highest standards, the entire team suffers.

HIRING THE RIGHT MANAGEMENT TEAM

Many of the criteria for hiring management is akin to hiring anyone for your company. Again, you want a clear connection to your company's culture. You look for solid communicators—applicants who say what they do and do what they say.

But the parameters for management go beyond that. You're also searching for people with a proven record of coaching who can inspire and adapt their style to various circumstances. That, like the leader at the top, requires a solid EQ and a genuine sense of empathy for those with whom they work.

Additionally, it's advantageous to hire people at all levels— management and otherwise—who display the potential to move up within the firm. They may express that interest in the application and interview process, or they may have a prior record of advancement. It's valuable to identify the motivation behind that desire. Perhaps someone wants to have a greater impact on a company culture they embrace or feel they can contribute in a role with a greater degree of decision-making. Money shouldn't be the primary motivator. It's far better that the desire is fueled by personal and professional growth.

I always look at new hires with a focus on advancement potential. Not only does it simply make sense, but I also know that at some point I'm going to want to replace myself and then move on. So I look for people who can step up to that larger role.

Hiring with an eye on advancement potential is also beneficial to company culture. If someone starts out in a particular role and moves up, they're that much more inculcated in the culture. They've seen it and worked with it in various settings, and they'll be that much more adept at inculcating others.

The ramifications of placing an ill-suited person in management can be fatal. As the Chinese general and philosopher Sun Tzu once noted, if a general gives a command and the soldier doesn't follow it, that's on the soldier. Should it occur a second time, the fault lies with the general. That's simply poor leadership.

FIRING EMPLOYEES

To be candid, there are very few people who don't mind having to fire someone. For them, it's just another part of the job. That's true. But for most of us, me included, it's perhaps the worst aspect of running a business.

But there are ways to mitigate the sting of the experience and frame it constructively. That starts with a simple rule of thumb. No one should ever be surprised when they're terminated, short of some unexpected or outrageous situation or behavior.

Attitude & Alignment with Mission

137

One way to approach possible termination is to look at various employees in terms of four quadrants. The fourth quadrant is the optimal one—"Rockstar," those who are doing their jobs very well with great attitudes. Keep giving them increased responsibilities.

The next group, quadrant two, might be occupied by employees who aren't performing up to their potential but who are great people and teammates. They're engaging, collaborative, communicative, and empowering. Take those people and try to develop them into Rockstars.

The last two are both difficult and easy. Quadrant one occupants—"Trouble," those who have a poor attitude and job performance—terminate ASAP. If they're doing well but have a poor attitude—"Challenge" quadrant—try to get to the root of the issue to help improve their attitude. Unfortunately, although performance can often be improved, poor attitude is a more difficult case.

Still, the decision to fire someone should only come after many interventions and attempts to address whatever may lead up to termination. Reviews, coaching, and warnings should occur in an effort not only to let a struggling employee know there are serious issues but to also let them know that you're willing to make every reasonable effort to help solve them.

Emphasize that the central issue is one of behavior, not the person. That unto itself can take much of the discomfort out of having to say they need to step up their game. Stress that their behavior or output simply isn't fitting in with the company culture.

Support is critical. Emphasize that you're on their side. You want them to succeed. If, however, they can't get there, that's OK, but they won't be able to stay.

As mentioned previously, lay out in detail what the employee needs to do. Tell them where they are now, where they need to be in the future, and how you're going to get them there.

But make it just as clear that if efforts at improvement fail for whatever reason, then you're very likely to part ways. That can head off future emotion-packed events.

In fact, by using this strategy, I've never once had to endure a firing that ended on a truly horrible note—slamming doors, screaming, crying. By the time we get to the point of formal termination, the employee understands that they were given every opportunity to improve. Termination seems the only sensible, albeit unpleasant, outcome. On many occasions the employee has actually apologized for putting me in that position.

Remember that you're not doing a subpar employee any favors by allowing them to stay on. It's not fair to the employee, their colleagues, and you as the head of the company. Tell them that you value them too much to simply kick the can down the road.

Express support for their postemployment situation. If you're comfortable doing so, tell them you'd be glad to help them find new employment. I've had ex-employees disappear for six months only to resurface and request references. That's more than just the decent thing to do—a former employee who knows that their dismissal was handled with dignity and compassion will let others know that you're someone who values respect for others. No one should feel humiliated or disrespected when you separate.

Years ago I read Jack Welch's *Jack Straight from the Gut*, where he describes having to fire 10 percent of General Electric's workforce. At the time it seemed way too hard-core, almost heartless. But as I thought about it longer and matured, I came to understand it. I realized that if you're just leading people on and allowing them to stay when their performance doesn't warrant it, at some point someone's going to say, "You're out." If you really care about the person, better to do that when they're younger and more employable instead of after years of subpar performance.

Much of great leadership comes from the gut. But not all, as I'll cover in the next chapter.

CHAPTER NINE

MANAGE METRICS

Recruiting and retaining topflight employees require a good deal of emotional intelligence. Knowing how to read someone else is definitely handy when working with talented people.

But managing people and other aspects of your business doesn't have to (and shouldn't) come solely from your gut. That's where metrics come in. When I started, I was a "gut-level" manager. It didn't always work, so I went back to school for an MBA and Six Sigma Black Belt. You don't need to go as far as I did to learn metric-driven management; you just need to keep reading!

Applying metrics to management decisions can provide an objective form of evaluation. By analyzing performance-related data, not only can you make better choices but, in so doing, you'll be a better leader. You're better positioned to handle your resources more effectively and to implement measures to correct problems or improve performance that much faster.

METRICS DEFINED

As you undoubtedly know, a metric is simply a numerical value that offers a form of objective measurement.

As a physician you are familiar with the value of data interpretation. Without that information and guidance, far too much of what we do every day would be left to more subjective observation—a valuable component, but also incomplete.

The same dynamic holds true with your business. By tracking, compiling, and evaluating various types of data, you're able to accurately assess various aspects of your business's operations, from systems development to individual job performance. That makes for better decision-making, better processes, and more engaged and fulfilled teammates.

This begs the question of what sort of metrics may be most valuable.

Google the term "business metrics" and you'll uncover dozens of suggestions about valuable metrics—everything from gross revenue to lead conversion to absenteeism. Some are very specific to particular types of businesses, while others are more universal.

Metrics are assigned to the "vertical" or particular niche in which your start-up fits. There are basically nine verticals that apply to most businesses. They are, in no particular order:

- Enterprise: Selling a service to a large enterprise (i.e., Citrix or Seagate Technology).

- E-commerce: Selling goods online (i.e., Warby Parker).

- Subscription: Selling a service to a consumer base (i.e., Blue Apron).

- SaaS: Software as a service. For example, selling subscriptions to other businesses (i.e., DocuSign or Slack)

- Marketplace: A company that acts as an intermediary between buyers and sellers (i.e., Airbnb).

- Advertising Company: A company that provides free services to consumers and derives revenue from advertisers (i.e., Instagram).

- Hardware: A company that sells hardware to other businesses or directly to consumers (i.e., Fitbit).

- Transactional: A company that enables financial transactions between two parties, (i.e., Venmo or PayPal).

- Usage-based: A company that is compensated every time a customer uses the service (i.e., an urgent care center).

It's beyond the scope of this book to cover all the metrics for each vertical. Instead, I'll limit this description to several recurring metrics used by most of these verticals.

- Monthly recurring revenue (MRR): This one is used for recurring services like subscriptions or SaaS businesses. The number does not include onetime or nonrecurring revenue.

- MRR compound monthly growth rate (CMGR): The implied growth rate between two months. CMGR equals the latest month MRR divided by first month MRR.

- Annual recurring revenue (ARR): How much revenue is recurring on an annual basis?

- Churn: How many customers have canceled subscriptions or stopped using your service?

- Paid customer acquisition cost (CAC): How much are you paying to acquire customers?

- Bookings: sum of all new customer contracts. This measures actual value of signed contracts, not letters of intent or verbal agreements.

- Total number of unique customers: How many customers are using your platform or service?

- Gross margin: (Total revenue minus cost of goods sold [CoGS]) divided by total revenue.

- Daily active users: For advertising companies this represents the total number of unique visitors in a twenty-four hour period.

- Monthly active users: Same as above, unique users active at least one time in the last twenty-eight days.

I helped develop a scorecard when we began building the urgent care business. This included every metric we were following. One obvious one was patient metrics—how many people were we seeing, and, just as important, how were those numbers trending? A further refinement to that metric is repeat customers—a telling statistic of end user satisfaction. About 50 percent of our business was return customers.

Another metric we tracked was door-to-door time—how long was the time frame from the moment patients walked into the building to the time they left? In an operation whose appeal lay in efficiency, this metric was a critical barometer.

But that particular metric also came with a caveat. While, on the one hand, we wanted patients handled efficiently, we also didn't want them to feel as though they were being rushed along on a conveyor belt. We addressed that by incorporating metrics such as patient satisfaction, as well as repeat visits. The goal was to find that sweet spot where patient loads were well handled but not at some needlessly breakneck speed.

While many metrics are specific to performance and procedural issues, metrics are also essential in finance. (I've covered this topic before, particularly in Chapter Seven, but it bears repeating.) For instance, one such metric in our urgent care business was net revenue per visit. We wanted to know just how much income each individual patient was generating—a key dynamic for a business geared to seeing large numbers of patients in the most efficient manner possible.

Other financial metrics include average number of days of accounts receivable, time between patient visit and when bills are mailed, and percentage of bills returned based on inadequate information. It makes financial management that much easier and accessible—your overall operation becomes very black-and-white as metrics readily identify areas where performance is improving and other areas that are chronic problems.

Another consideration with metrics is an outlier—statistics or data that seem too good to be true or, worse, are inexplicably poor. That can skew analysis quite a bit. Two patients whose visits each last ninety minutes can throw off a much larger group whose door to door is considerably lower.

To counter that, it's advantageous to track metrics systematically and acquire sufficient data over a meaningful time frame—at least six months, if not longer. By identifying an average culled from extensive information, we could pinpoint and dismiss any outliers that were simply too extreme to be realistic, let alone useful.

We also examined a provider's efficiency using relative value units or RVUs. An RVU measures the amount of work necessary to achieve certain outcomes. This metric allows you to determine how efficiently care is being delivered. As you know, you can see five young patients with pharyngitis in the same amount of time it takes to manage a stroke patient or one with multisystem problems.

Metrics can also be effective in evaluating marketing or public outreach programs. In the private autopsy business I mentioned earlier, we sent out notices to mortuaries to let them know we were available should relatives wish to have an autopsy performed on a loved one. Correlating that campaign with the number of responses we received was a way to gauge the program's success—a form of paid CAC.

We also compiled a metric that measured how quickly we were able to complete an autopsy from the time we received a job request—a key barometer of efficiency. A similar metric measured how long it took to complete the actual autopsy procedure. Lastly, we established a metric that tracked time required to generate a final report. Our goal was two to four weeks; however, the time it took to receive the pathology report was beyond our control.

Metrics can be tailored to the specifics of a business—another attractive feature. For instance, at Tribal EM, our metrics include tracking of shifts filled, nursing and physician revenue, and all service providers' average hourly income rate.

The beauty of metrics is that they apply to all types of businesses, not just healthcare-related ones. For instance, retail outlets routinely track metrics such as foot traffic levels, time spent in the store, percentage of people who actually purchase products, and the number of returns. The same holds true for advertising campaigns—an easy metric to track with coupons and other materials.

I started a business called Find Urgent Care, an advertising website that helped prospective patients find urgent care centers close to their homes. While it was free to patients, we charged urgent care centers a monthly fee for listing on our website. Here we evaluated our MRR, churn, and paid CAC.

WHAT TO TRACK, HOW OFTEN

Metrics are also inherently flexible.

There are certain metrics that are critical to particular types of businesses. For instance, there probably isn't a retail operation anywhere that doesn't follow foot traffic and other gauges of customer flow and activity. Likewise, a virtual business that operates primarily online is going to follow click-through rates, origins of customer traffic, and other aspects of who's coming to the site, where they came from, and what they're doing once they're there, as well as the other metrics I detailed above.

But it doesn't have to be so cut-and-dried. With metrics, it's also a question of what you deem relevant and what has an impact on the business in both positive and negative ways. For instance, an increasingly popular metric tracks Yelp reviews and other online customer feedback.

The time frame in which metrics are compiled also matters. The general rule of thumb calls for monthly collection, in part to avoid statistical anomalies that can occur within shorter time frames.

In addition to the problem of outliers, shorter time frames can also produce little usable analysis. For instance, if I see five patients every day for a week, it's likely I'm going to receive great customer feedback given the time I can allocate to each. But that daily average doesn't reveal much about patient satisfaction. However, monthly metrics that include days with much heavier patient traffic paint a more accurate picture of customer service. Did the quality of patient care suffer on particularly busy days?

That illustrates how metrics allow a business owner to make reasoned adjustments based on what the numbers say. Collecting a longer train of data can reveal meaningful patterns, such as particularly busy times when patient loads generally spike. Knowing that, the business owner can implement corrective measures, such as added staff on certain days where patient turnover might otherwise slow down, impacting revenue.

THE BALANCED SCORECARD

Another valuable concept to understand about metrics is the interplay between them.

For instance, a physician may be the most empathetic provider possible. She takes her time with each patient, letting them go into as much detail as they like about their health issue and taking time to comprehensively explain what treatment she is recommending and why. That sort of thoughtful attention is inevitably going to produce high patient satisfaction metrics.

However, other metrics may suffer. For instance, a physician who takes more time is likely to generate less revenue than another doctor who is caring and efficient. Additionally, a slower service provider may inadvertently impact feedback from other patients who are waiting to be seen.

That illustrates the value of what I call a balanced scorecard. By that I mean the overall picture that various metrics show when they're examined in conjunction with each other. With the physician I just described, that may suggest continued emphasis on compassion but perhaps greater attention paid to the length of the visit. Taking all metrics into account allows for a complete, balanced overview of your business and the ramifications of changes in procedures and practices.

A balanced scorecard also reveals whether the business is in fact living by its stated values and mission statement. For example, an urgent care operation that stresses compassion may inadvertently sacrifice that to undue efficiency. Lacking metrics to gauge adherence to certain values can make them essentially worthless. And consumers quickly notice a business that sacrifices its values, even unknowingly.

But metrics go beyond philosophical applications. They also serve as a guide to optimized decision-making, employee management, and pivots in strategy and operations.

> Taking all metrics into account allows for a complete, balanced overview of your business and the ramifications of changes in procedures and practices.

MANAGING TO THE METRICS—PROCEDURES AND PEOPLE

The beauty of metrics is that they offer an empirical basis with which business owners can make critical decisions, impacting everything from procedural issues to employee performance.

With regard to procedures, metrics can identify and quantify both positives and problem areas with work routines, how customers are treated, and other central issues. For instance, your metrics may identify unduly long customer wait times. That, in turn, can be addressed by boosting staffing levels or changing the way staff greet and direct customers.

As a real-life example, the amount of time required to record patient background and information at our urgent care centers was problematically long. We solved it by installing self-check-in kiosks. Prior to being seen by a staff member, patients checked themselves in and entered their medical history. When the provider saw them, more than half of the necessary chart was done, allowing the staff member to zero in on specifics and, ultimately, treat the patient that much sooner.

As an added benefit, patient feedback on attention and compassion also improved. Since the provider didn't have to compile a chart from square one, they were free to spend more time with patients addressing their concerns and answering questions in detail.

But again, metrics aren't limited to procedural issues. Metrics also allow leaders to objectively review employee performance and, from there, recommend strategies for improvement. To that end we approach this in ways that may strike some as unusual.

First, we review every employee's scorecard every month. Employees are divided into three color-coded groups—green, yellow, and red—signifying, in order, those who are performing well, those facing challenges, and employees with serious performance issues. The color-based system offers an easy-to-understand and convenient way to keep employees informed, using empirical statistics rather than just subjective management feedback.

Additionally, all employee scorecards are made public. That may seem needlessly forthright to some—putting out all results, good and bad, for everyone to see—but our employees have been uniformly positive about it. For one thing, they treat it as a competition (an attitude that I hoped they would adopt). They want to know where they stand in relation to their peers.

A group focus also comes into play. By compiling data and identifying trends, we can pinpoint employees working effectively and those whose performance is more of an outlier (for both good and bad).

For instance, we may compile information about total time spent with a patient. Those falling at either end of the spectrum—too little or too much time—can be identified and the issue addressed. Staff falling somewhere in the middle are getting it right—not too long but not hurried either.

Additionally, we offer bonuses to top performers. However, it's clear to me that money isn't the primary motivation. Since employees are ranked in relation to others, professional pride also plays a significant role. No one wants to be seen as an inadequate teammate.

Further, we look to leverage top performers. We designate them as coaches and mentors for struggling colleagues. That improves overall team performance while further cementing camaraderie around a commitment to improvement. There's a real sense of a rising tide boosting the quality of work of the group.

Again, the overall program is very transparent. By dividing the group into three sections, those in the bottom third are made well aware their struggles may compromise their long-term future with the company. Stay there too long and it may prove necessary to begin the formal series of reviews and warnings that could ultimately lead to dismissal.

The system is just as forthright with processes. Should an area of operations prove problematic for an extended time period, we may conclude that it's the process itself that's at fault. In those cases, we may go back to square one to examine whether a certain process or system needs to be reworked or abandoned. Those are opportunities for company-wide improvement, not just improvement of one particular individual or area of operations.

Ultimately, managing to the metrics boils down to a few simple rules of thumb. First, we keep nothing secret about metrics. From there, based on those metrics, we identify employees whose performance should improve. Lastly, we provide all tools possible to help struggling employees through coaching or reworking a troublesome process or system.

RAPID PROCESS EVALUATION

Given that data is most effective when tracked consistently, metrics allow business owners to make significant changes very quickly. This is called rapid process evaluation.

Rapid process evaluation is akin to a minimum viable product—an idea or system that's introduced on a limited basis for examination and possible implementation on a larger scale. Rapid process evaluation allows business owners to test out changes suggested by metrics and from there gauge their effectiveness.

> Given that data is most effective when tracked consistently, metrics allow business owners to make significant changes very quickly.

Here's an example. No one enjoys the helpless, aggravating feeling of sitting endlessly in a waiting room. To address that, we introduced what we called the "no-waiting waiting room."

Patients made appointments online in the usual manner but didn't actually come to the office until we telephoned them to let them know their scheduled time was approaching. We nicknamed it WAHOO, an acronym for wait at home or office.

Patients arriving at their specified appointment time were immediately brought into the exam room. It really was a complete upending of conventional care sequencing—waiting room, front desk, waiting room, triage, exam room. Instead, we effectively brought care to the patient, rather than the patient navigating an often inefficient and frustrating process.

We tried that out at several locations. Patient satisfaction went up, door-to-door time went down, and documentation improved. We also began to make our waiting rooms small, cutting down on the amount of non–revenue producing space—a classic example of a minimum viable product that warranted greater implementation.

That's the basis of rapid process evaluation. It allows you to test things quickly. Then, go back to the metrics. Those numbers will tell you whether a new process is working, if it needs tweaking, or if it's simply not workable. It's a great way to test out new ideas and evaluate them empirically, quickly, and inexpensively.

Lastly, when looking for ideas for metric analysis and, ideally, rapid process evaluation, don't just consider similar businesses. Possibilities that can ultimately improve your metrics are all around you, provided you keep both your eyes and mind open. For instance, the idea of self-check-in kiosks at urgent care centers first came to me when I saw a similar system in place at Disney World.

The same holds true for employee performance metrics. For instance, a restaurant I go to often consistently offers great food and friendly, attentive service. Intrigued, I eventually asked the wait staff about their training. I learned all about their employee shadow program, in which recent hires followed and observed experienced staff.

The result: NextCare University, where we trained people for weeks before they ever set foot inside our urgent care clinics. The connection was clear—if that restaurant could ensure a great dining experience through a particular training program, we could certainly replicate that in healthcare.

Urgent care and restaurants may seem miles apart. But there are metrics with crossover value that are relevant for both.

Metrics can also be of enormous benefit when developing and evaluating your public outreach efforts, including marketing, advertising, obtaining media coverage, and other promotional steps. That's what we'll cover in the next chapter.

CHAPTER TEN

PROMOTE YOUR BUSINESS

A number of years ago, we were busy opening multiple urgent care centers throughout the Denver area.

A grand opening was planned for each location, with all the attendant publicity we could muster. This included a number of large, very expensive canvas signs, placed at strategic points along various streets to boost visibility.

One morning I was driving into the city to check on the centers and happened to notice that several signs were missing. I was both upset and confused. Who would want some oversized banner advertising medical care?

I had my answer soon enough. As I passed by a bench, I saw one of the missing banners—a sleeping bag for a homeless person.

I quipped that at least he was putting it to good use.

That's a representative illustration of advertising, public relations, and other forms of public outreach. What seems an ideal strategy to connect your business with the public can end up going in a completely different direction—one that may not be conducive to attracting the marketplace's attention.

For start-ups and small businesses, it's useful to understand not just the nuts and bolts of public outreach but also what makes them successful. That's why instead of focusing on the specifics of advertising and marketing, I'm going to focus on elements and components that truly work. Hit those marks and the nuts and bolts will largely take care of themselves.

ONE CRITICAL GOAL: EDUCATION

In 2015 a major telehealth company opened its doors—a direct competitor with my own telehealth business, MeMD. The company was a formidable rival, with financial resources that we couldn't even come close to matching. In fact, they reportedly dropped $1 million just on their go-to market strategy. They released a series of commercials that were very well done.

All I remember thinking was *I'm screwed*. MeMD was just five years old and barely scraping by. I was all but certain that they would knock us off the map.

They were out of money and bankrupt within one year.

That was both good and bad news for me. On the one hand, what seemed to be a formidable competitor had quickly disappeared. That was the good news.

The bad news was the resulting uncertainty. If those guys couldn't connect with the public with all that money, how would I ever be able to?

Then I realized that the general public simply wasn't ready to accept the idea of virtual doctor's visits. Even with these really clever ads and a great marketing company behind them, it simply didn't work. That hinted at the missing component—education.

I've come to understand that any successful effort to connect with the market—be it through advertising, marketing, or other sorts of programs—needs to include a significant element of education, particularly when the concept is new. It's simply critical that any outreach effort show consumers why something is a good value and how they as end users will benefit

Never assume the public has an understanding of your business.

Much of what I've done as an entrepreneur, and what many others have done as well, is start businesses that are foreign to many consumers—even revolutionary. Think Uber, Airbnb, and others—now largely accepted, but back when they started, consumers approached them with a mix of confusion and wariness. They simply didn't know what to expect, and perhaps more importantly, what pain points those businesses could potentially solve.

> **Never assume the public has an understanding of your business.**

That's why education is of such overriding importance. Advertising and marketing that proclaim, in so many words, "Here we are; come check us out!" don't inform or persuade. They merely announce. And if consumers don't understand the substance and value of what's being announced, even the slickest of messages can fizzle.

My various businesses had a lot of solid advertising campaigns back in the day, although we didn't employ expensive broadcast advertising to the extent that our defunct telehealth competitor used. In addition to the banners/bedrolls I mentioned, we used direct mail and door hangers, as well as billboards and radio messages. Those campaigns inevitably incorporated some form of call to action, such as a coupon or code that could be used for a free flu shot or a sports or school physical.

Those proved very effective. For one thing, we demonstrated both our purpose and value through complimentary services. And once we were able to get target customers into the facility itself, we could offer in-person education regarding who we were and why they should consider using us again. We were able to move past the challenge of educating from a distance. They could now experience our great customer service firsthand.

To summarize, education is often absent from marketing and advertising programs. By assuming consumers know all about a product or service and why it's a good value, companies jump over an essential step. Instead, they devote a great deal of money to involved campaigns that are professional and well executed but ultimately misdirected. And many new businesses and start-ups don't have that cash to spare.

That's why I feel the best and most cost-effective advertising and promotion comes via public relations directed at the media. It's relatively inexpensive, naturally tuned toward education, and open to replication. Getting press is probably the best form of early marketing and advertising—where your time, effort, and money are best directed.

But it takes legwork.

OBTAINING PRESS COVERAGE

Attracting media attention is a multistep process. Treat it as you would business development, as though you're pounding the pavement on the hunt for new clients. It's a slow, constant push. Approach it in that manner and it's much easier to get your arms around.

First, determine whom you should contact. If your competitors are receiving press coverage, look to see who's writing about them. Who are the media people—newspapers, magazines, television, blogs—who cover your segment of the industry?

This used to be less of a chore. Back in the day, I knew all the reporters in the Phoenix area who covered various healthcare segments, all the different magazines and newspapers. Since our start-ups were more focused geographically, a search was that much easier. Now it's more of a challenge, not only because of the number of people who report on healthcare but also in the number and variety of media outlets.

Still, no matter where a particular reporter or contributor happens to be, it's important to try to develop a close relationship with them. By far the best way to accomplish that is by way of a personal introduction—ideally from a fellow entrepreneur. Having a mutual acquaintance can quickly establish a sense of trust and validity between you and the media person.

Here's another area where many business owners, particularly newcomers, make some common mistakes. First, they assume that sending out emails to a massive list of media contacts will connect them with at least one interested person. Known by the phrase "pray and spray," it's outreach's equivalent to cold calling, and just about as effective. Volume doesn't ensure success—without the common reference point that personal introductions can afford, huge email campaigns likely land in a reporter's or editor's trash file moments after they arrive.

Another pervasive misstep is reaching out to the media without anything of value to offer. You can send a reporter an email saying your product is the coolest new thing since cell phones, but that's not necessarily newsworthy. Rather, you need to offer something of substance and value—both to the media person and the reader or viewer who may ultimately get to see it.

What's newsworthy? Product launches are newsworthy—something of importance is coming out today. But don't just leave it at that. Explain why the new product is valuable, what its goal for the end user might be, or how it addresses some sort of widespread pain point or common problem. Explain why it's timely.

It never hurts to sweeten the offer. Dangle the possibility of an exclusive or ask the journalist to embargo the story until the date where the new product or service actually hits the streets.

Here's a tip: if you choose the exclusive route, best to target a media source with a sufficiently large following to make excluding other outlets worthwhile.

Milestones are also newsworthy. It was certainly newsworthy when MeMD claimed its one millionth subscriber. Landing a big deal or partnership is also newsworthy, such as when we partnered with the supplemental insurance carrier Aflac. We put out press releases and contacted journalists in the healthcare and IT industry to point out the agreement's ramifications.

Fundraising goals can also be highly newsworthy. When we closed our Series B round, we let others know. Not only does that signify success; it's also implicitly a form of education. If a company is worthwhile enough to attract significant financial backing, there likely is something there of value. That can warrant further investigation, both from the media and consumers themselves.

A sense of timeliness is critical to certain forms of media outreach. For instance, in the heart of the COVID-19 pandemic, MeMD announced our Return to Work program. This eventually attracted some thirty thousand business subscribers and detailed how various businesses could develop and implement a systematic and safe in-house program to get employees back to being productive on-site. I can't imagine a timelier story for the media, one that at the same time informed the public as to what we were all about in terms of healthcare.

SOME MORE DOS AND DON'TS

Connecting and nurturing contacts with all types of media are a proven, cost-effective way of connecting with the consuming public. Here are a few additional suggestions to make the most of this strategy:

- Again, don't spray and pray. Sheer volume doesn't equate to success. You're likely wasting your time and resources and, just as importantly, potentially annoying useful contacts.

- Don't badger media contacts. Don't call up repeatedly and say, "Do you have ten minutes to talk?" Deadline-driven journalists rarely have time to spare. Reaching out without any substantive basis for doing so will make them reluctant to share what little time they may have.

- Treat them with respect. Tell them how much you value their cooperation and coverage. When applicable, give them exclusives.

- Don't bullshit them. It will inevitably come back to haunt you. It's OK to make things seem a little better or more provocative than they might be, but never exaggerate to the extreme. Nothing ends a relationship between a journalist and sources faster and more completely than inaccurate or unreliable information.

- Never bad-mouth competitors. Like the job interviewee who claims he can do whatever he wants when giving notice, needlessly criticizing others only makes you look petty.

- Work to establish a regular cadence in the timing of press releases and contact with newspeople. That doesn't mean sending out a press release or checking in with a reporter every week. But several press releases within a few months or letting them know when something noteworthy has taken place can help keep you top of mind.

- Stay in touch. Once you have a relationship, keep it vibrant and current. One person I know at the local business journal just celebrated her thirtieth work anniversary with the paper. I made certain to offer my congratulations. The personal touch can help make lifelong friends and colleagues, some of whom may actually reach out to you: "Hey, John, what's your take on this story? What angle would you pursue?" That makes for a two-way street, each of you serving the other's goals and needs.

OTHER MODALITIES

Public outreach should also have a significant component of visibility.

Accordingly, give due consideration to vehicles such as YouTube, as well as your company website.

We did a bit of YouTube marketing with MeMD. We offered videos that had some animation in them, as well as live actors and shots. They were very effective in helping to educate consumers about telehealth's advantages and benefits. By incorporating visuals, you're showing rather than merely telling what your company is all about.

Moreover, research has shown that visual material is far more likely to be shared with others than mere text. That helps build word of mouth, referrals, and other essentially cost-free means of spreading the word. Developing a business that's self-propagating is obviously preferable to repeatedly spending money on new customer acquisition.

Using YouTube, as well as other visual mediums such as Facebook and Instagram, also lets you perform A/B testing—a concept I discussed earlier. Here you compare two versions of a particular form of outreach to gauge which is the more attractive and successful. You can experiment with elements such as appearance, words, colors, and other components to see which gets a better response.

The same holds true for your website. Like all your marketing, advertising, and other aspects of your outreach, it should be geared toward helping visitors understand and appreciate your company. Keep it simple, straightforward, easy to navigate, and make sure to offer something of value. That can be introductory service discounts or promotions tied to newsletter subscriptions or some other form of ongoing contact. Make value as synonymous with your brand as any other aspect of your business.

A newsletter or other sort of regular communication can be exceedingly effective in educating consumers. It offers you the chance to develop an extended narrative, allowing you to go into detail about services, products, or general education. That, like ongoing media contact, builds a regular stream of communication that supports long-term relationships and loyalty.

CUSTOMER SERVICE RECOVERY

It may not seem like marketing, but customer service recovery is a central element of how you convey yourself to the marketplace.

Customer service recovery refers to steps to correct a problem or bad experience a customer may have had. First, understand and accept that disappointing customer experience is an inevitable part of business. Never assume that your business is so well functioning that no customer will ever have a subpar experience. It's going to happen.

In the internet era, bad customer experiences can quickly go viral with meaningful impact. A 2018 study by PowerReviews found almost 100 percent of consumers consult product reviews when making purchase decisions, up from 95 percent only a few years prior. More than a quarter of those shoppers consult reviews for every online purchase.[4] That makes customer recovery efforts critical in terms of word of mouth and how customers view your business.

> Never assume that your business is so well functioning that no customer will ever have a subpar experience. It's going to happen.

Here's an example of the import of customer recovery. When I'm dining at a restaurant, I almost never send bottles of wine back—maybe twice in my entire life. One time I ordered what I was certain would be an excellent cabernet. This particular bottle was terrible. I tried to send it back.

Moments later the bartender came to our table and took the liberty of pouring himself a glass. He announced it tasted fine. I disagreed and ordered another bottle. When we got the check, we saw the restaurant had charged us for both bottles, even though the first was completely undrinkable.

That experience showcases two realities. First off, no one in the restaurant even acknowledged our opinion of the first bottle. By saying it tasted fine, they were effectively saying our opinion was immaterial. That impression was only furthered when they charged us for the first bottle, even though we only took a couple of sips.

I've never returned to that restaurant. I've also shared that experience with many friends and colleagues. Not surprisingly, I later learned that that restaurant had gone out of business—hardly a shock.

On the other hand, I've patronized many restaurants that rarely slip up with their food and their service, but it does happen. What

---

4   "The Growing Power of Reviews," https://www.powerreviews.com/wp-content/uploads/2018/03/The-Growing-Power-of-Reviews.pdf.

do they do? For one thing, they validate your experience. Often the meal is completely comped.

Further, they offer a complimentary dessert.

In other words, they own your bad experience. They take full responsibility and, further, go the extra mile to do whatever's necessary to make a poor meal seem like an isolated incident, rather than business as usual.

That's a great customer recovery—something we spend a great deal of time on. While that's obviously important to all businesses, it's particularly critical in healthcare. Accordingly, we address that proactively. For instance, after a visit, we always place follow-up calls: "How was your visit? Are you getting better? Is there anything more we can do for you? Is there anything about your visit we could have handled better?"

Marketing via customer follow-up and, if necessary, recovery is as important an element in public outreach as any other marketing. Not only does it convey our commitment to excellent care and correcting any mistakes, but it also offers an opportunity to upsell: "Hey, if you know anybody who needs a school physical, please send them our way. We noticed that you haven't gotten a flu shot yet; we noticed that you have not scheduled your mammogram." People genuinely appreciate that type of concern and attention level—again, something of value.

With regard to marketing and public outreach, mistakes, poor service, and other issues don't have to be disastrous. It all depends on how you approach them and the attitude you convey to customers.

IMPATIENCE AND THE "LONG TAIL"

One final consideration with all forms of outreach is what's referred to as the "long tail."

The long tail addresses the timeline associated with marketing, advertising, and other public contact. Basically, it's a form of caution—the reality that it will likely take a long time to produce meaningful, positive results.

That can head off frustration and counterproductive impatience. It's not just a question of sending out a press release and waiting for the customers to start rolling in moments later. Rather, it's about systematically building communication and outreach steadily over a long period of time. By consistently letting the marketplace know you're there to serve and offer genuine value, you're at the top of mind when what your business does connects with consumer needs—whether that's bandaging a cut finger or having a menu suited to celebrate a college graduation.

That's why it's critical that you as the founder remain directly involved in all forms of public outreach. Moreover, staying close to all efforts to connect with the market underscores the importance of building personal relationships with media and others.

As you grow and your business becomes more complex, it may be prudent to hand these issues off to a PR agency or some other like professional. But when you're just starting out, it's valuable for the founder to be involved not only in the planning and execution of outreach but also in developing the sort of long-term, personal relationships that can be invaluable as your business grows and matures.

CONCLUSION

Congratulations, you've made it to the end! I hope what you've learned has inspired you and boosted your confidence in your ability to successfully build the business you've been dreaming of. I know that you have what it takes to create the next product or service that will change the world—or at least improve the lives of those who use it.

In this final chapter, I am going to discuss and review some of the most salient things I've learned over more than twenty-five years of starting both successful and unsuccessful ventures. We've already addressed some of these concepts; some are common sense, and some will surprise you, I'm sure.

Always remember that start-ups are hard. There is no easy way around it. I tell myself often, "If it were easy, anyone could do it." You are here because you are not just anyone. You have the idea, the desire, the drive, and the tools to pull it off. However, even with all your attributes, start-ups are difficult.

When starting a new business, it's crucial that you never take your foot off the gas. Momentum is everything. Once you lose it, it's hard to regain. While that may not bode well for work-life balance—at least in the beginning—to really be successful, you must maintain momentum.

Remember, this is a marathon, not a sprint. Any of you who have run a marathon know this. No matter how badly you want to stop, the key to finishing is to simply keep running despite everything.

> You are here because you are not just anyone. You have the idea, the desire, the drive, and the tools to pull it off.

In short, you need to work like hell. For me this meant eighty to one hundred hour workweeks for years. Approach it this way—if you're working eighty to one hundred hours per week, you'll accomplish in four to six months what takes others a year. It sounds brutal, but success does have an associated price tag. The simple fact is, start-ups are demanding and require countless hours to be successful.

One key trait I've recognized in myself and in others who become successful founders is that they're obsessed with what they're doing. With pretty much every company I've started, I find myself thinking about it morning, noon, and night. While it can become all-consuming, it still doesn't feel like work. If you do not feel obsessed, you have picked the wrong product or service.

Founders are also eternal optimists who are still grounded in reality. The balance they achieve is that they are willing to face cold, hard facts and still believe they can and ultimately will be successful. They have the ability, like Marcus Aurelius, to let the thing that was once the obstacle become the way. Thus they rejoice in any and all challenges.

Additionally, you must have a tolerance for failure and the pain that comes from it. There will be many times after the initial excitement wears off when things don't go as planned. You're forced to dig deeper to stay positive, to keep moving forward, and, most importantly, to remain focused. A high pain tolerance is a must have for start-up founders.

The tolerance for pain goes hand in hand with seeking criticism. A question you will need to repeatedly ask others is "How can I make my product or service better? What should we be doing to better satisfy our customer's needs?" The responses may not leave you feeling very upbeat. Thus the ability to absorb the pain, refocus, and pivot as necessary is paramount.

One thing that I've noticed over the years is that when the proverbial shit hits the fan, successful founders resort to action. It is easy but ultimately unproductive to wallow. As Theodore Roosevelt said, "In any moment of decision, the best thing you can do is the right thing, the next best thing is the wrong thing, and the worst thing you can do is nothing." Never do nothing. When the chips are down, act. These are often the times that lead to the biggest breakthroughs, the largest epiphanies. When you are forced by circumstances to get creative, know that successful founders find inspiration in challenges and respond in previously unrealized ways.

Starting a new venture also requires a certain degree of risk tolerance. As I discussed throughout the book, it is risky to invest your time, money, and effort into an unknown. The good news is that as a physician, you will always have the ability to put food on your table and a roof over your head. So, at the end of the day, understand that although you may be accepting a certain degree of risk, you will always be able to provide for your family.

Finally, founders absolutely love what they're doing. I describe it this way: I haven't worked a day in my life because every day I wake up and do what I love doing most—building something that improves the lives of others. Again, if you don't love what you're doing, you've probably picked the wrong thing upon which to focus.

When trying to figure out if a product or service is the "right" one, ask yourself: Is it so compelling that people tell their friends about it? I relied on this with MeMD. I thought the service was so revolutionary that it would spread organically by word of mouth. It did, but only to a point.

Also, the product or service should be very easy to explain and understand. The more complex it is, the harder it will be to convey your message. With HealthyBid, the explanation was simple. HealthyBid allows patients without insurance or with high deductibles to solicit bids from providers for elective and nonemergent diagnostic tests and procedures. When I explain a new venture to people, I look for their eyes to light up. With HealthyBid, they inevitably did.

Is what you are doing part of an emerging trend? Will it soon see exponential growth? Are you sensing that the world is making a fundamental shift and that your product or service is riding on the front of the wave? With SlideSmart (the online platform to sell medical slides), I sensed that the days of slide carousels were ending. From then on all educational material would be presented digitally. It seems like a given now, but at the time, the thought of doing a lecture and not walking in with a slide carousel was nearly heretical.

Another key question: Is what you are doing something that will be "huge if it works"? Even if the chances are small, a product or service that will scale incredibly quickly and is part of a growing trend will be worth the risk.

Additionally, make sure you earn enough money for yourself and enough to reward your investors. In my career, I've had some start-up ideas that I thought were great opportunities; however, I was not quite sure how I would monetize them. Ultimately, I just didn't know how to get a return on my investment.

An important advantage that start-ups have over larger companies is that they're nimbler. They can bring things to market much more efficiently and for far less cost. They can adjust faster. Remember that when you are worrying about competing against a larger, more experienced, and better funded competitor. A quote from Steve Wozniak is on point: "All the best things I did come from not having money and not having done it before." I always remind myself of this when I'm concerned that I've started something for which I am ill equipped and undercapitalized—which happens to be most everything I've done.

One final thing I learned is that many ideas initially sound odd or even bad, yet those are often the ones that turn out to be the biggest winners. Generally, it's because no one has contemplated the idea before, so, as a result, it sounds really far out there. MeMD fit into this category. Some people I shared the virtual health concept with seemed to get it. However, most said, "That will never work" and then proceeded to list all the reasons why. It's important to listen to their points and then address them in your product or service. As for MeMD, it's been a long road, but it has in fact worked.

As relevant as all this is, the most crucial quality for you and your company is benevolence. Simply be kind. Be kind to your customers by treating them fairly and compassionately. Be kind to your vendors by paying their bills in a timely manner. Be kind to your employees by going out of

> One final thing I learned is that many ideas initially sound odd or even bad, yet those are often the ones that turn out to be the biggest winners. Generally, it's because no one has contemplated the idea before, so, as a result, it sounds really far out there.

your way to care for and about them, holding them to high standards and then rewarding them when they exceed expectations. Finally, be kind to yourself by getting enough sleep, exercising, and eating well.

Still, all this requires money. When raising money, the best pitches are the simplest ones. Here's what I'm trying to do, and here is why it's so compelling. Here's why I am the person to do it, and here's what you'll get if you join me for the ride.

Once you have raised your equity round, keep your investors informed. No surprises. I've invested in a couple of companies where despite reaching out, I heard little or nothing for eighteen months or so, only to receive notice that the company was out of business. Don't do that to your investors. Often they are a great resource for much more than capital. Use them for their networks and guidance, and keep them informed.

Above all, remember that the fun is in the journey. If it all works out, all of your efforts will be well worth the difficulty and your exit will be exciting and lucrative. However, I promise you that it won't be the exit that you will remember most. It will be the good times and bad that you endured along the way and all the learning and everything else that came with the intense effort.

A quote I refer to often when things get difficult is again from Theodore Roosevelt:

> It is not the critic who counts; not the man who points out how the strong man stumbles, or where the doer of deeds could have done them better. The credit belongs to the man who is actually in the arena, whose face is marred by dust and sweat and blood; who strives valiantly; who errs, who comes short again and again, because there is no effort without error and shortcoming; but who does actually strive to do the deeds; who knows great enthusi-

asms, the great devotions; who spends himself in a worthy cause; who at the best knows in the end the triumph of high achievement, and who at the worst, if he fails, at least fails while daring greatly, so that his place shall never be with those cold and timid souls who neither know victory nor defeat.

When you start your own company, you too will experience "great enthusiasms" while daring greatly to change the world. You've got this.

JOHN'S 21 RULES
(AND COUNTING)

1. Kindness always.

2. If it were easy, anyone could do it.

3. Rejoice in the obstacles.

4. To improve it, measure it.

5. The faster you go, the slower the clock goes and the longer you live.*

6. You will never hit a target you haven't identified.

7. Don't predict the future, create it.

8. Success is one step past failure.

9. Fall seven times, get up eight.

10. If you think you're hurt, you are. If you think it's hard, it is.

11. Never waste a crisis.

12. Multiple projects create multiple opportunities, which lead to multiple successes.

13. If it can be finished in a year, it can be finished in a month.

14. When you think you've given it your all, you still have more.

15. Protect your downside with multiple streams of income.

16. You promote what you permit, and you get what you incentivize.

17. "No" is just a word.

18. If no one is dying, how bad can it be?

19. Passion, persistence, and culture trump strategy.

20. Eat right, get plenty of sleep, drink lots of fluids, and go like hell.**

21. Always be the calmest person in the room.

*Peter Diamandis
**Nike

STARTUP CHALLENGES

I actually consider this a non-success rather than a failure at this point. I was asked by a couple of friends who are chiropractors to partner with them. The business model involves billing for services following a physician-approved treatment plan; Medicare reimbursement is higher and they will approve more visits.

I started with focusing on what I know how to do: look at the literature to see if chiropractic treatments had shown any benefit (they do for back pain and headaches). The next step was to see if their model was above board with Medicare (it is). I then looked at what my role would be. I would need to review and approve care plans and make sure the patients were improving with the care they received. The vision was that our model would be successful and, due to other chiropractors struggling, we would be able to swoop in and buy their practice for pennies. We would hire the current owner as an employee, pay them more than they were making before, and institute our model. We would then make enough money to pay the current chiropractor and have some substantial profits for ourselves.

Everything looked great and I jumped in. I made sure we had a contract setup that included our corporate structure and everyone's liabilities and responsibilities. We put together a solid contract and corporate structure. I thought I was ready to sit back and make sure my bank account was big enough to handle all the money that would be coming my way.

Four years in and our business is still above water but not doing well enough to expand; in fact, we closed one of our three locations. Some of the things I have learned:

Just because something is above board with Medicare doesn't mean they are going to gladly pay every claim you send them. There were numerous deficiencies in our charting and billing. It has taken over a year to organize and refine our notes and process to be fully compliant with Medicare. We were never doing anything fraudulent, we just didn't chart the way we were supposed to in order to get fully reimbursed.

Being a good clinician does not necessarily translate into being a good administrator/business leader. It is a different world. The business world has its own language and culture. Instead of just ordering specific diagnostics and therapeutics to treat a patient, business has accounting, advertising, and competition analysis, all of which you need to know and understand in order to diagnose and treat what is ailing the business. It needs to be learned, studied, and practiced. You can't make money off of good ideas alone.

It is difficult to find the right people to help. We assumed we would be able to find chiropractors that were both good clinicians and motivated to learn our model of care. We went through four chiropractors at one of our locations but none of them worked out. We ended up closing that location. We also thought we would be able to find someone who could take over the day-to-day operations of managing employees, billing, customer complaints, and accounting. No such luck. They are still being managed by the partners.

Daniel Bishop, MD

PERSONALITY AND CULTURAL
FIT IN THE WORKPLACE

F ounder passion and determination are the fuel for start-up companies. That passion enables a founder to wear many hats and solve a myriad of problems encountered in start-ups. However, at some point, as the company grows, founders must give way to trained professionals to manage areas where the founder lacks expertise. The first hire is usually a manager who eventually assumes the CEO role and performs any necessary duties required for the good of the company. Slowly, other professionals are added to the team.

The first CEO is an extremely important hire and can make or break a company. As a founder, I searched, networked, identified candidates, and did due diligence on a set of CEO candidates. After many interviews and countless phone calls, I was finally "all in" on the first CEO hire. I had confidence that I had chosen a bright, smart, energetic CEO who shared my vision and was willing to do battle alongside me.

In hindsight, I erred in managing our first CEO. As expected, this person was extremely smart, talented, and determined and shared the vision of growth of the company. Yet, he slowly showed signs of poor team skills. I had vouched for his team-building skills with reference calls and interviews with his former teammates. I was confident that this was just a "stressful" time and that the team would meld soon. Month after month, quarter after quarter, the team was replete with internal strife. Daily there were raging fires that needed to be extinguished; these fires were interpersonal issues, not issues related to the building of a start-up company. Our organization's cohesiveness and teamwork were simply broken.

Adamant about my CEO choice, and fully behind him, I was blind to the reality of the situation. The team was fragmenting. Key people in the organization were pointing out the problem. Other team members were threatening to leave the team. Yet my fog didn't clear. I continued to be the cheerleader of a team that was imploding.

My error was not recognizing that the talented CEO that I had backed wasn't the right guy for the job due to a lack of team cultural fit. The lesson here for people who are assembling a team is to do the due diligence on a hire, back them up, assist, and help them in any capacity, but also to be clear headed and recognize when that person is not the right fit. When necessary, there is a duty to step up and resolve the situation or, if there is no resolution, then there is a duty to put the right person in the leadership positions before the team falters.

Lloyd P. Champagne, MD
Co-Founder, ExsoMed

DEVELOPING THE BUSINESS MINDSET

After months of looking for the perfect location, hours of negotiating the terms of the lease, and tens of hours spent designing the space with an architect, it was time to sign the contract. This was the major first step and commitment to our new business and I had worked hard to get it perfect. Then, an email came letting me know that they were giving the space to another business with "all their financials in place."

My brain came up with this conclusion almost immediately: You are not a businessman; this was doomed to fail from the start. With that, my entrepreneurial career was over before it ever started. For the next two weeks, I laid aside years of preparation for this business and countless hours of work and started looking for jobs.

Now, I use this story to teach my patients some of the principles of cognitive behavioral therapy (CBT). The authors of CBT have illustrated ten to fifteen common faulty thought patterns that lead us to erroneous conclusions. They call these patterns cognitive distortions. Two of the common cognitive distortions are personalization and over-generalization. With personalization, you blame yourself for something you weren't entirely responsible for. Though I certainly had an influence on whether or not that deal went through, I found out later that there was a personal conflict between my broker and the owner that probably had more influence on why the deal fell through. At the time, however, I was sure this was all my fault and that it revealed a permanent flaw. Overgeneralization views a negative event as a never-ending pattern of defeat, which is what I saw ahead of me due to this one event.

Ultimately, I realized that whether these fears I had about myself were true or not, I was not willing to give up on this dream and now

I have been in business for over four years. Though the business has grown beyond my expectations and has an even brighter future, I am trying to use measures other than outward success to drive my behavior. Businesses will fluctuate and come and go, but my goal has become to work and act based on values. There will always be someone more capable or more successful than me, but I will move forward because I believe in working hard to do good for others.

Kendrick Johnson, DO

A FAILURE AMONG A CAREER OF SUCCESS

D ear Colleagues: The following narrative is an example of a less than optimal outcome (failure) regarding participation in an opportunity to grow a "Medicare Advantage Primary Care Network" with a prominent New York–based private equity firm in the recent past.

I have spent twenty-plus years in this field since Medicare Risk became "mainstream" as the Medicare Advantage program. Our firm has helped insurance, hospital, and physician organizations grow their Medicare Advantage (MA) programs from virtually zero to in excess of one million dollars on several occasions.

When approached by a large, reputable NY-based private equity firm to sit on the board of directors of a new company we shall call "ABC Physician Network Inc.," I agreed. The primary reason was that I was extremely familiar with the Medicare Advantage business, the chairman of the board was a close friend, and the private equity firm was established and well financed. In addition, I was chairman of the quality and compliance committee with clear line of sight to many areas that may go astray of regulatory Centers for Medicare & Medicaid Services (CMS) requirements.

At the first board of directors meeting, it became apparent that the private equity firm management had arbitrarily purchased a group that they felt could be the nidus for growing the rest of the network without regard to all the variables that make an MA plan successful. It is common knowledge that 20 percent of physicians drive 80 percent of the revenue in an MA plan and this major criterion had not been appreciated.

By the end of the first year it was clear that the fifteen physicians from the initial acquisition (the acquisition was approximately ten million dollars) were not clear on how to optimize care in an MA environment and had lost an additional three million dollars. The chairman of the board stepped in and tried to right the ship. He put into place HCC (severity of care modifiers) improvement methods, HEDIS domain process improvement, incentive payment initiatives, etc.

All efforts were correct but the physician culture and quality of clinical care were not there from the start. As a result, in the second year, the group lost an additional five million dollars. The private equity firm, instead of merging this underperforming asset with another proprietary asset, which is commonplace in the private equity world, decided to double down on its unsuccessful efforts. It was clear that this strategy was probably not going to work and the chairman resigned. Approximately six months later, the private equity firm closed down the company and took a loss of approximately twenty million dollars, blaming the board and management for their inability to turn this company around.

My educational takeaways from this less than optimal experience:

Evaluate first and foremost the private equity or other financing source behind any venture you involve yourself with and their track record in the area they are asking you to participate in.

Do not join the board of a venture just because you have faith in the chairman, as they may not have control of the business or be the ultimate decision maker.

Even being chairman of an important board committee (in this case quality and compliance) does not necessarily give you "line of sight" as to what is really going on operationally.

Most private equity firms will not shut down an investment without transferring some of the asset into another related company. This did not occur in this case.

Be very suspicious and careful when the private equity firm, in advance and without subject matter expertise, creates the revenue engine that will determine the success of the venture.

This is one small example of a "failure" that has educated me versus many successes that in some cases I took for granted. However, I hope some of these insights will be of benefit to someone potentially looking at a similar opportunity in their life going forward.

Jacque J. Sokolov

ACKNOWLEDGMENTS

This book would have remained on my endless "to do" list but for the help of some amazingly talented individuals. Thank you Jeff Wuorio for your diligence and expertise in helping prepare this manuscript. Thank you to Kaleigh Shufeldt, Tiffany Youtchoko, Amy White and Rene Beckham for your constant patience, editing skills and persistence in bringing this to fruition; I would not be here without your help and guidance. To the amazing team from Advantage|Forbes—Kristin Goodale, Carson Kendrick, Stephen Larkin, Alison Morse and Alec Stubing—thank you for all of your support and guidance through this process.